FLEXIBLE PACING
For Able Learners

Neil Daniel Texas Christian University
and
June Cox Gifted Students Institute

A Product of the ERIC Clearinghouse on
Handicapped and Gifted Children

Published by The Council for
Exceptional Children

Library of Congress Cataloging-in-Publication Data

Daniel, Neil, 1932–
    Flexible pacing for able learners / Neil Daniel, June Cox.
       p.   cm.
    "A product of the ERIC Clearinghouse on Handicapped and Gifted Children."
    Bibliography: p.
    ISBN 0–86586–183–8
    1. Gifted children—Education—United States—Case studies. 2. Individualized
instruction—Case studies. 3. Educational acceleration—Case studies. I. Cox, June,
1919– . II. ERIC Clearinghouse on Handicapped and Gifted Children. III. Title.
LC3993.9.D36 1988
371.95'0973—dc19

                                      88–21014
                                         CIP

A product of the ERIC Clearinghouse on Handicapped and Gifted Children.

Published in 1988 by The Council for Exceptional Children, 1920 Association Drive, Reston, Virginia 22091–1589.

Stock No. 328   Price $12.50

This publication was prepared with funding from the U.S. Department of Education, Office of Educational Research and Improvement, contract No. 400–84–0010. Contractors undertaking such projects under government sponsorship are encouraged to express freely their judgment in professional and technical matters. Prior to publication the manuscript was submitted to The Council for Exceptional Children for critical review and determination of professional competence. This publication has met such standards. Points of view, however, do not necessarily represent the official view or opinions of either The Council for Exceptional Children or the Department of Education.

Printed in the United States of America.
10 9 8 7 6 5 4 3 2 1

Contents

About the Authors

Neil Daniel is Professor of English at Texas Christian University where he has directed summer sessions with the Gifted Students Institute for superior students at middle and high school levels. He has, in addition, conducted summer institutes for teachers of honors and Advanced Placement English. Daniel was one of the writers of the Richardson Study (*Educating Able Learners*) and has written on education of the gifted for such journals as *Roeper Review*, *G/C/T*, and the *Bulletin* of NASSP.

June Cox is Executive Director of the Gifted Students Institute. She directed the Richardson Study and was the primary author of the final report of that study, *Educating Able Learners: Programs and Promising Practices.*

Kathleen Martin is Associate Professor in the School of Education at Texas Christian University. For 3 years she has worked closely with the Pyramid Project on staff development in mathematics education. Her research interests include the development of learning environments that enable children to encounter powerful mathematical ideas.

CHAPTER 1

Introduction

In a previous publication (Cox, Daniel, & Boston, 1985, p. 135) we suggested that allowing students to move ahead on the basis of mastery may be the most important means of providing adequate opportunity to all students. We called for flexible pacing to accommodate differences in learning styles and learning rates among school children. Here we explore how flexible pacing is being used, particularly with students of high ability, in schools and districts around the United States. We believe that educational change is made possible and will lead to improvement if those responsible for school policy and instructional practice have an opportunity to see what others have done and can select from a range of tested options.

A particular challenge of this study is that no uniform set of terms describes the educational options we have explored. What one school calls "continuous progress" another school names "mastery learning." The program that employs various means to accomplish flexible pacing may be called an "accelerated program" or described as "extended learning." A single label such as *ability grouping* can identify several quite different instructional arrangements (Slavin, 1987). In our program descriptions we tried not to be misled by apparent similarities and differences that turn out to be a function of the terms used. Part of our goal in this short book is to help redefine the words we use in this relatively uncharted domain of public schooling.

We define *flexible pacing* as any provision that places students at an appropriate instructional level, creating the best possible match between students' achievement and instruction, and allows them to move forward in the curriculum as they achieve mastery of content and skills. For able learners, flexible pacing will generally result in some form of acceleration, accomplished either by moving students

We define flexible pacing as any provision that places students at an appropriate instructional level, creating the best possible match between students' achievement and instruction, and allows them to move forward in the curriculum as they achieve mastery of content and skills.

up to advanced content or by moving advanced content down to the students. In practice, flexible pacing can be achieved by a variety of methods (see Figure 1):

- **Continuous Progress.** Students receive appropriate instruction daily and move ahead as they master content and skills. The purest form of flexible pacing, continuous progress breaks the age-in-grade lockstep.

- **Compacted Course.** Students complete two or more courses in a content area in an abbreviated time.

- **Advanced Level Course.** Students receive course content normally taught at a higher grade level.

- **Grade Skipping.** Students move ahead one or more years beyond the next level in the normal sequence of promotion.

- **Early Entrance.** Students enter elementary school, middle school, high school, or college earlier than the age usually prescribed.

- **Concurrent or Dual Enrollment.** Students at any grade level may take classes at the next school level. For example, elementary school students take classes at junior high; junior high students take high school classes; high school students enroll at a college or university.

- **Credit by Examination.** Students enter an advanced level course or receive credit upon satisfactory completion of a comprehensive examination or upon certification of mastery. The best known examples are the College Board's Advanced Placement and College Level Examination Program, which give credit at the college level, but credit by examination is frequently offered at the high school level.

In principle, flexible pacing is not limited to students of higher than average ability. The rate of progress can be varied in either direction. In the best of worlds all students would progress through their schooling at a pace that provides steady challenge without crippling frustration or unreasonable pressure. Insofar as each child has a unique

FIGURE 1

Flexible Pacing Umbrella

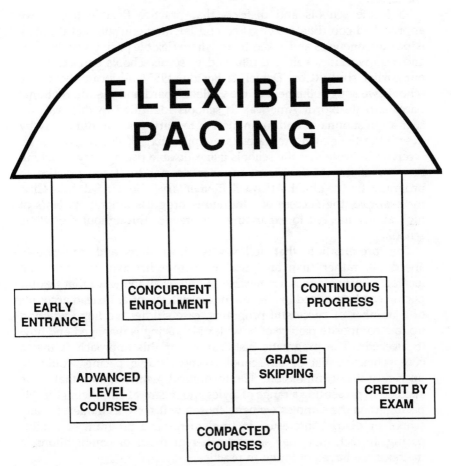

style and pace of learning, each would be grouped with different students from period to period, day to day. The generalized curriculum for any schooling unit, whether class, school, or district, would be a complex of individual learning patterns, a cable made of many strands.

For the sake of this work we confine ourselves to flexible pacing offered to students of demonstrated high ability. We have found that flexible advancement through the district's regular curriculum is an option offered, if at all, most often to students of the highest ability. The increased benefit of allowing students to advance at their own pace is most apparent among the most able. Such students are likely to be frustrated or to spin their wheels in the generalized age-in-grade lockstep that characterizes most schooling in this country. They are also likely to capitalize on flexible pacing by showing dramatic progress and by exercising their options for increased educational challenge.

To locate schools and districts that practice flexible pacing we approached coordinators of gifted and talented education at the state education agencies and asked them where flexible pacing was in place and was working well. We returned to some schools singled out in our earlier study (Cox, Daniel, & Boston, 1985). To locate secondary schools we sought the help of the College Board and the International Baccalaureate North America. To schools identified in this way we sent a questionnaire and an invitation to participate in our study by describing their own programs (see Appendix A). The responses we received indicate that the schools using flexible pacing vary widely in their practices. A significant number do not limit the practice to programs for the gifted. At Lowell Elementary School in Salt Lake City, for example, the success of continuous progress among students of high ability has led to expanding the practice throughout the whole school.

The presentation that follows is descriptive and consciously anecdotal, rather than analytical or comprehensive. We have not located all schools that use flexible pacing or all the ways that flexible pacing can be realized in a school or district. We offer instead accounts of a number of successful programs, case studies we hope will add up to a composite picture of how flexible pacing is managed and how it succeeds. The pragmatic justification for this approach is that a comprehensive list of all schools using flexible pacing would be unwieldy if not impossible. The theoretical justification is that if we succeed in presenting a range of styles and means of employing flexible pacing, then the samples we have chosen will serve as models for any school or district interested in implementing a program of flexible pacing. In fact, they may suggest other methods or combinations of methods we have not found in practice.

Some unevenness in our treatment results from our method of gathering information. We have relied on what the schools and districts told us. Aside from the subjective element introduced by self-appraisal and the absence of experimental controls to provide comparison, we have found little uniformity in the ways individual schools practice and evaluate flexible pacing. And of course the language used to describe flexible pacing varies from place to place. We are satisfied, however, that from this process of self-reporting a pattern has emerged. We are confident that our profile of flexible pacing is fairly complete. We hope the information we have gathered will be useful even without experimental data.

An additional limitation arises from the time-bound nature of our report. The picture we present is broad but instantaneous. Many of the schools and districts we cover have been using flexible pacing in some of its forms for only a year or two. Their programs have almost certainly changed since the respondents returned our survey. The best that we can claim for this study is that it represents, within the limits of our abilities, the state of flexible pacing as it was being practiced in the 1986–1987 school year.

In the interest of providing the most instructive examples of flexible pacing in operation we concentrate on whole districts or schools in public systems. While there is much to learn from the experimental lab school with a selective population, we suspect our audience will be more interested in what works in the public, tax-supported domain.

After describing the diverse means of achieving flexible pacing in practice at the various levels, we include three sections we hope will be especially useful. Chapter 6, on Cooperative Programs, highlights a small number of programs that are not located in individual school districts but cross the boundaries between districts and illustrate the special benefits of cooperation between agencies and across institutional lines. Chapter 7, Selected Features of Flexible Pacing, shifts attention to the elements required to design and implement a program built on flexible pacing. And a special chapter by Kathleen Martin illustrates how a continuous progress approach might be developed in a single discipline.

This brief book has many authors. We have had enthusiastic cooperation from a large number of schools and districts. Teachers and administrators have provided useful information on short notice. In some instances the descriptions have been incorporated with only minor editorial revisions. Those who contributed to this project are listed in Appendix D. Special thanks are due, as well, to Judith Kelly and Elene Ondo, who read the manuscript during its preparation and offered useful suggestions. Paul Brinson was a great help with background research. Lisa Lock spent hours on the phone tracking down contributors to verify details. Jane Hellums designed the figures used to illustrate the text. We assume full responsibility, however, for any errors of fact or interpretation we may have inadvertently introduced.

CHAPTER 2

Historical and Theoretical Context

Flexible pacing is an alternative to the most widespread arrangement of students in our schools, grouping by age, one grade per year of chronological age. Arrangement by grades was introduced at the Quincy Grammar School, which opened in Boston in 1848. This pattern, admired and advocated by Horace Mann, was a significant advance in schooling at a time when our population was shifting from rural areas to urban centers. Students in large numbers could not be accommodated practically in single rooms or in the three divisions (primary, grammar, and high) that had replaced the one-room school in more populous centers.

The newer arrangement linking school grade with age, one room for each grade, became the standard in cities and towns large enough to support multi-room schools. The graded curriculum was an outgrowth of graded schools. It offered the practical advantage that no single teacher was required to master all subjects at all levels.

The graded school was not seriously challenged until the 20th century. It has not been displaced on a wide scale to this day, although most educators agree with Madeline Hunter (1964) that expecting all children the same age to learn from the same materials is like expecting all children the same age to wear the same size of clothing.

Early in the 20th century, dissatisfaction with the high rate of failure in our schools, coupled with the influential educational philosophy of John Dewey, led to a reassessment of the inflexible, grade-a-year arrangement of our schools and particularly to a challenge of the implicit assumption that all youngsters of the same age have the same learning ability. Educators with an increasing concern for individual differences among students attempted to structure schooling to address those differences. A parallel concern, that education in our

*Some way of arranging students so that they
can move at a comfortable pace is needed.*

schools should provide for the total person, not only the academic achievement of individual students, provided an argument in favor of age grading. The goal was to find an arrangement that would foster social interaction among children of the same age as it provided steady academic challenge at rates suitable for different abilities.

One way of accommodating the variable learning rates among children of the same age was the ability grouping commonly referred to as "tracking." Under the tracking system children of similar ability, as measured usually by IQ or achievement test scores, were grouped together in high, middle, or low classes and moved through the curriculum at a fast, moderate, or slow pace. In tracking's best known model, the Detroit Plan developed in 1919, the groups were referred to as X group, Y group, and Z group (Morgenstern, 1966, p. 11). The objections raised by critics of this plan were that tracking typically remained a lock-step plan, moving pupils in blocks through the sequence of "grades," and that the grouping was usually based on generalized ability rather than on specific aptitude or demonstrated progress in particular subject areas (Goldberg & Passow, 1966).

Another adjustment to individual learning rates led to the development of totally individualized programmed learning packets, in widespread use in the early 1960s. Elementary students worked through packets prepared for them by teachers and aides. The students needed little instruction and were not required to wait for their classmates before moving on to the next packet. Many children responded favorably at first to this opportunity to move at their own pace. Over time, however, students became bored with solitary learning, and teachers came to resent the paperwork that consumed instructional time. As Julian Stanley has suggested, even able students are slowed down by programmed instruction (Stanley, 1979, p. 36).

And yet some way of arranging students so that they can move at a comfortable pace, neither rushed on before they can master a concept nor held back by slower learners, is needed. Many methods have been tried. Robert Slavin's review of research on grouping offers a typology of grouping methods in current use (Slavin, 1987). The various types are separated into between-class grouping and in-class grouping and include regrouping for selected subjects, such as reading and math. Several of these methods result in flexible pacing, for they allow students to move through the school curriculum at rates determined by achievement rather than age. The key is flexibility. If schools adopt ability grouping, Slavin suggests, students must be able to move from group to group as their levels of achievement warrant. In our judgment, many students should be in different ability groups for different subjects. Without such flexibility, a tracking system may doom the first grader who gets off to a slow start to a high school career of choices limited to the lowest level of classes.

Among challenges to the grade-a-year arrangement of students, the most ambitious and the most carefully documented is the nongraded school. In a historical review of the nongraded movement, R. I. Miller (1967) reports that in 1961, 12% of American elementary schools had some nongraded sequences in place. By 1964 as many as a third of the the school systems surveyed by the NEA Research Service (441 school systems with enrollments of 12,000 or more) had one or more elementary schools with a nongraded sequence. Miller makes it clear, however, that even in 1967 nongraded schools were regarded as experimental and were seldom widespread in a given district.

The names most closely identified with the nongraded school are John Goodlad and Robert Anderson. Their book, *The Nongraded Elementary School* (1959) remains the primary text for educators who embrace the concept. In 1960 Anderson and Goodlad surveyed practices in 89 communities in which some 550 nongraded schools were reported. Their analysis of this survey discloses a major difficulty of controlled research in the area of graded and nongraded schools. Many teachers in nominally "nongraded" schools continue to use "graded" practices and have "graded" goals. And in graded schools many teachers attempt to individualize instruction and "to soften the effects of grade organization in their work with children" (Anderson & Goodlad, 1962, p.72). Research on graded and nongraded schools is likely, therefore, to rely on self-appraisal and subjective reporting. Our own study shares this limitation.

Because our study focuses primarily on flexible pacing for students of high ability, the practice of adjusting the pace of instruction to the needs and capabilities of individual students generally leads to acceleration. A single student or perhaps a small group of students, capable of mastering the material of a given unit faster than others in the class, are allowed to move on to the next unit and so get ahead of their classmates. If the student is moved ahead to work with older students in a higher grade in one or more subjects, the result may be grade skipping, concurrent enrollment in two or more levels, or early entrance into the next higher institution. As an alternative the student may be kept in a grade with students the same age but allowed to study curriculum content from a higher level. In some situations students carry on advanced work in one or more subject areas by correspondence, in Saturday classes, or at summer sessions (Sawyer, 1984; Stanley, 1979).

At one extreme among the means of accommodating the needs of unusually able learners is the radical acceleration introduced by Julian Stanley in the Johns Hopkins Study of Mathematically Precocious Youth (SMPY). As Stanley describes it, SMPY is "resolutely interventional, longitudinal, and accelerative" (Stanley, 1979, p. 29). The striking advancement of a relatively small number of students, highly gifted in math, has dramatized that once students are freed of their grade boundaries, they thrive on the challenge of appropriate pacing. A similar program for verbally gifted youth (SVGY) is in place at Johns Hopkins. Stanley recognizes that students learn at different rates in various subject areas and has argued that children should be grouped according to their achievement level in a given subject area (Stanley, 1980). Concentrating on the area of his immediate concern, he has suggested that students should be taught mathematics by longitudinal teams of mathematics teachers (K–12) who would facilitate the movement of students along a continuum of mathematics skills and topics at a pace dictated by individual abilities, regardless of grade. Chapter 8, by Kathleen Martin, Toward Improved Instruction for Mathematically Able Students, suggests how such teams might be developed but does not argue for radical acceleration.

Not all educators agree that the best way to meet the needs of a fast learner is to allow students to move through the curriculum at a rapid pace. The position of the National Council of Teachers of Mathematics, cited by Martin, is that superior students should move at a faster pace and should be allowed to explore a wider range of concepts, with adequate substance, as they move through the graduated curriculum. NCTM argues that such students have a right to increased rigor and higher demands than those set for more nearly average students. The schools and districts we surveyed have a range of enrichment options for students whose learning pace allows for exploration.

Acceleration and enrichment, moreover, need not be mutually exclusive alternatives. In a discussion of varying learning environments, Gallagher (1985a) mentions both the acceleration of the Johns Hopkins programs and the enrichment options favored by Renzulli (Renzulli, 1977). Our position is that enrichment must be integrated into the school curriculum so that it does not lapse into unrelated activities. Moreover, to be meaningful, enrichment must be geared to the student's needs and abilities. In such a case appropriate enrichment activities will be accelerated. Under ideal conditions every student with higher than average learning abilities would be offered enriched acceleration and accelerated enrichment. The Model Mathematics Project covered in our chapter on Cooperative Programs illustrates how such a mix can be achieved.

---

*Every student with higher than average learning
abilities would be offered enriched acceleration
and accelerated enrichment.*

In a cautionary article, Joyce VanTassel-Baska points to a number of pragmatic and political difficulties that interfere with flexible pacing (VanTassel-Baska, 1985). Because flexible pacing stretches the traditional organizational structure of our schooling, it requires retraining and extensive adjustment for school personnel. It appears to conflict with the egalitarian and democratic philosophy that undergirds our commitment to universal education, for it implies that children are not intellectually equal. Moreover, flexible pacing inevitably leads to grouping students of different ages. Because of a deeply entrenched commitment to social development as a function of public schooling, the continuing legacy of John Dewey, both parents and teachers may be suspicious of this practice. We are uncomfortable mixing students of different ages despite abundant research (Daurio, 1979; Kulik & Kulik, 1984) that students are better adjusted socially when they are given appropriate educational content, regardless of the age of students they are grouped with, than when they are grouped with age-mates and not offered a sufficiently challenging curriculum.

The graded school was an important development in American education, an improvement in efficiency necessitated by the industrial revolution and a shift in the distribution of our population. In recent decades the electronic revolution and corresponding demographic changes have made other adjustments in our educational system not only possible but necessary. It is our hope that flexible pacing, in its various forms, will help us make use of expanding educational technology and our best understanding of current social needs to serve all students well.

Our look at schools that practice flexible pacing has enabled us to examine a variety of administrative arrangements that permit students to move forward on the basis of their mastery of the skills and content in the school curricula. We start with the premise that the best education matches the pace of instruction with individual abilities, and we have seen that many schools have made important strides in the direction of achieving that ideal. In our conclusion we will try to pull together what we have learned and suggest ways to increase the pace of improving education.

CHAPTER 3

Flexible Pacing at the Elementary Level

In our sampling of flexible pacing in elementary schools we begin with continuous progress, the most complete form of flexible pacing. It is the showcase option. But as this chapter makes clear, there are various ways to provide a sound match between the students' achievement and the levels of instruction.

LOWELL ELEMENTARY SCHOOL, SALT LAKE CITY, UTAH

Two discrete but complementary programs at **Lowell Elementary School** help us to illustrate continuous progress and also deal with an issue in flexible pacing mentioned in the introduction. While we believe flexible pacing is the ideal educational mode for all students, for this study we are most concerned with the ways flexible pacing works among students of higher than average ability. Lowell Elementary School has employed continuous progress for able students in the academically accelerated extended learning program since 1977. At the time of reporting, the district's program was identified by the acronym EQUIP (Educational Quality by Understanding Individual Potential). The success and manageability of flexible pacing in the extended learning program has led to the adoption of continuous progress throughout Lowell Elementary School.

Designed for students who learn at a faster rate and who would profit from a varied curriculum and individualized teaching, EQUIP serves 188 of the 479 students in the school. Students in EQUIP are grouped by ability rather than by age or grade. The three major divisions, designated Form I, Form II, and Form III, are generally

---

*Help of parents and other interested volunteers
enables the school to offer many
enrichment experiences.*

---

planned for ages 5–7, 8–11, and 12 and over. Children may move from form to form, however, as development and achievement indicate. Forms I and II are in the elementary school building; Form III is located in a high school.

The major emphasis of the Form I curriculum is on reading, language, and mathematical skills. The basic curriculum in all Form I classes is taught at least one year above grade level. A yearly study theme enhances the curriculum and is incorporated into reading, social studies, science, art, and music.

The basic curriculum for Form II is also taught one year above grade level. Students, ability grouped for instruction, use the Open Court mathematics and reading programs, supplemented with other programs for levels above sixth grade. Mathematics levels range from fourth grade through algebra, and above when needed. The reading/language arts program levels range from fourth grade through high school. Heavy emphasis is placed on writing skills, problem solving, and thinking skills.

The foreign language curriculum in the Lowell program begins with French in kindergarten through second grade and includes German and Spanish from grade three. Students are grouped in two or three levels per language on the basis of their abilities.

An important element in the extended learning program is parent volunteer participation, called "co-oping." The district encourages parents with children in EQUIP to provide teachers with at least 3 hours per week of cooperative assistance. The help of parents and other interested volunteers enables the school to offer many enrichment experiences to extend the regular curriculum. We will return to this element of the Lowell Elementary School program in our chapter on selected features.

Principal Keith Langford, reporting for Lowell Elementary, describes the academic benefits of the full-time extended learning program as tremendous. Highly accelerated learners, he points out, are able to spend a full day every day learning at an instructional level that meets their unique needs. To illustrate he cites the case of Matthew, a fifth-grade student, being taught high school geometry. As a second grader Matthew was taught pre-algebra and as a fourth-grader he

*Placement is determined by which style of
teaching best meets the needs of the learner.*

learned algebra. At the time of writing, plans were being made to place Matthew with a university mathematics professor for instruction during his sixth-grade year.

The program offers equally important social and emotional benefits to its students. Many have not fared well in regular classrooms. In the EQUIP classes they are surrounded by learners like themselves who may share the same interests as well as abilities. No longer "outsiders," they function as group members. Indeed, says Langford, they now have the opportunity to feel and act like children, rather than like miniature adults.

A more recent program at Lowell Elementary School is its Continuous Progress Program, a nongraded approach to instruction in which all other students of the school, those not in EQUIP, are grouped in multi-age levels rather than in grades. Students are assigned to teams of teachers rather than to one teacher. One team teacher serves as a student's homeroom teacher. Each homeroom has students whose ages span 2 to 3 years. The grouping in teams and subgrouping within teams are based on the students' mental, physical, emotional, social, and educational development as well as on age. Determination of the group is based upon the judgment of teachers and administrators developed through observation, assessment, and formal and informal testing. Placement in the subgroups is determined by which style of teaching best meets the needs of the learner, in what peer group the student is likely to work best, and what level of difficulty in each subject area seems likely to elicit the best work.

In reading, language arts, and mathematics students are grouped according to their academic abilities. If a learner functions ahead of or behind the level of others in a given group, the student is moved "up" or "down" to a more appropriate group. In all other areas of the curriculum—science, social studies, art, music, and physical education—student grouping is based on interest, attitudes (self-concept, motivation, etc.), skill level, and past experiences.

Continuous progress requires careful management and coordination. The teaching teams and the administrators have weekly scheduled meetings and frequent unscheduled meetings to discuss student placement and progress, curriculum, and schedules. Individual folders on each student document the students' progress in each subject area. These folders move with the students from team to team. Students leave Lowell's Continuous Progress Program to attend a graded intermediate school (7th and 8th grades) before going to high school (9th through 12th grades).

Although students in the Continuous Progress Program are not selected for the competitive and academically accelerated EQUIP program, Keith Langford points out that some achieve well beyond the levels accommodated by the regular curriculum. For example, three students in the upper team (9–12 year olds) have been placed in the pre-algebra class taught in the full-time extended learning program for gifted students. This crossing between the two programs at the same school is an additional benefit for students at Lowell Elementary School.

Langford balances the example of the accelerated math students with another of a 6-year-old student who was reading at the third-grade level. To keep the child with others reading at the same level required shifting her to a team made up mostly of 8 year olds. Although she could succeed academically with the new team, she was emotionally behind her new classmates. The student was returned to her original team, and her teacher designed an individual reading program to foster academic growth while her team placement facilitated her emotional growth. The commitment to flexible pacing ensures that her learning needs will be met in the most appropriate classroom setting.

OTHER ELEMENTARY SCHOOLS

As the history of the Lowell Elementary School in Salt Lake City suggests, flexible pacing options, especially continuous progress, are often inaugurated with a limited population before they are instituted as a systematic provision for all students in a school or district. Among the schools and districts reporting to us, continuous progress has typically been introduced as a special provision for the most able learners, the gifted and talented. In the Governor Wentworth Regional School District, New Durham, New Hampshire, continuous progress is in place at the **New Durham Elementary School,** but only for 10–15% of the students (18 students in a school of 180 in 1987). According to Marcy Mager, the school's principal, New Durham School (K–6) has several advantages: the school is small, the principal is committed to G/T education, most of the staff members have received some G/T training and are committed to special programs for the gifted, and the community approves and supports the program for its most able learners.

*Since there is teaming of teachers between
grades, movement between grades is possible
and occurs for a few students each year.*

All students at New Durham Elementary are grouped for instruction in reading and math. Since there is teaming of teachers between grades and every adult knows every child, movement between grades is possible and occurs for a few students each year. Most often children are grouped within their own classes, all of which are heterogeneous. Every class has at least one group functioning above grade level; occasionally a child 2 years or more above grade level will be instructed alone.

The flexible pacing commitment at New Durham Elementary reaches beyond continuous progress to supplement the regular curriculum in various ways. For exceptionally able readers the program is a combination of group instruction 1 or 2 years above grade level two or three times a week, individualized reading programs and accompanying projects using trade books, and close attention to the writing process. Writing provides built-in continuous progress because it is intrinsically self-paced and children necessarily perform at their own levels. Advanced readers in upper grades also read with younger children, serving as mentors and directing projects for their younger counterparts. In mathematics as well, the abler students have their work compacted and engage in enrichment activities, advanced computer work, work on the next grade level, or mentoring for younger advanced children.

In the science curriculum earth science, biological science, and physical science are taught in every grade. The social sciences—geography, history, sociology, government, and economics—are taught in grades 1–6. Each unit contains specific mastery objectives and projects and open-ended activities to allow advanced performance within the unit. If a student demonstrates unit mastery at the beginning of a unit, the student is provided with an advanced set of experiments, projects, reports, or assignments. Because all units are carefully worked out and have been developed by school-wide effort, it is easy to move a child into the next area of study or to provide lateral enrichment at an appropriate pace.

Another school that offers continuous progress as an option for able learners is **Friendsville Elementary School** in the Garrett County Public Schools in Maryland. Since the early 1980s, Friendsville

Elementary has used continuous progress to meet the special needs of able learners, but not only those who are highly gifted or talented. In 1986–1987 continuous progress was provided for about 25% of the school's students (48 of 199). Selection of students is based on test scores as well as on the professional judgment of the teachers. The teachers consult with parents and advise them of the possibility of placing their child in the program of continuous progress. These discussions include a careful consideration of the child's academic achievement as well as the child's social and emotional development.

Teachers in the K–5 school are arranged into three cross-grade teams to facilitate flexible pacing. Teachers in each team meet at least once a week to discuss curriculum and to consider the achievement of each student. Because of the open nature of the school and the constant communication between staff members, continuous progress is available to all students in the school, although not all students are recommended for this option.

To illustrate the success of the flexible pacing options at Friendsville Elementary, Principal Jane Fox cites the situation of 8-year-old Christina, who was promoted from grade two to grade four. When she was in grade two, Christina needed instruction in reading at third-grade level. Christina was therefore moved to the third-grade classroom for reading, and she remained there for English and language arts. Comfortable with the third-grade curriculum and at ease with the other children in the class, Christina did well. At the end of the year the teachers consulted with Christina's mother and decided to promote Christina to the fourth grade. At the time of Fox's report, Christina was working at fifth-grade level in reading and math. In a team area that housed both fourth- and fifth-grade classes, she was able to work at her instructional level while remaining with a class of children she knew well. Fox reports that Christina is proud of her achievements and experiences no problems as a result of her double promotion.

A similar approach in a different physical arrangement is provided at the Irving Alternative School, in the Sioux Falls, South Dakota, Public Schools. This school, in existence since 1974, was designed to offer continuous progress for all its students (108 at the time of reporting). The alternative school has the full approval of the school board, and its philosophy and its educational program are reviewed carefully every year by the parent-teacher organization. Parents elect to have their children attend the Irving school and have the option of returning their children to the neighborhood schools at any time. The school has an enrollment cap determined by space and staff available; a waiting list indicates strong parental interest.

Goal setting and contracting are used in reading and mathematics. Irving teachers involve parents in the classroom to manage daily or

---

Teachers involve parents in the classroom to
manage daily or weekly goal setting and
for small group instruction.

---

weekly goal setting and for small group instruction. Reading and math unit tests are monitored by the principal, who keeps centralized records. In addition, each teacher maintains individual records to follow students' progress in Sullivan Programmed Reading, Houghton Mifflin Reading, and Houghton Mifflin Mathematics. Standardized tests include Slosson SORT, Metropolitan Kindergarten, Cognitive Abilities, and the Iowa Test of Basic Skills (ITBS). Teacher-made curriculum materials and tests are used in science and social studies.

The cumulative effect of continuous progress is illustrated by the case of Matt, a fourth-grader at Irving Alternative School. Matt entered Irving at the suggestion of his preschool teacher. He was already reading when he entered kindergarten and showed unusual ability in mathematics reasoning. Matt progessed through the programmed reading series and through addition and subtraction while he was in kindergarten. By second grade Matt was working in third-grade materials and in the Unique Learning Experiences program, which provided for horizontal growth by way of enrichment experiences in areas of interest to him. As a third-grader Matt worked with a high-school-age tutor in computer skills as mathematics enrichment. By April of his third-grade year his academic progress as measured by the Iowa Test of Basic Skills showed a grade equivalent of 5–4, with reading at the 84th percentile and math at the 91st percentile. While Matt's achievement would not place him among the highly precocious, he has profited from the flexibility of the Irving Alternative School.

So far we have concentrated on schools with small enrollments and schools that employ flexible pacing with selected populations. That flexible pacing works for whole districts and is appropriate for students of diverse abilities can be illustrated by a school district and a school that employ continuous progress for all students in a single subject area, mathematics. The **Montgomery County Public Schools** in Maryland have had the Instructional System in Mathematics (ISM) in place since 1977. The result of a cooperative effort by teachers, students, specialists, and administrators, ISM provides a graded series of objectives that make up a common curriculum from kindergarten through pre-algebra. The curriculum is divided into 18 levels to be covered in 9 years. Although objectives and assessments are

---

*The Instructional System in Mathematics
specifies a standard of mastery for each objective
so that student progress at different schools and
in different classrooms will have essentially the
same meaning.*

---

standardized, the system depends on classroom teachers to plan and use appropriate instructional methods. According to the district's "General Overview of ISM," submitted by the elementary math coordinator, new concepts should be related to old, subsequent skills should be anticipated, and periodic reviews should reinforce previously learned objectives.

A subset of the mathematics program objectives is designated "key objectives." The number of key objectives is kept to a minimum to make assessment and reporting as efficient as possible. It is important for teachers to teach additional, non-key objectives and so extend, reinforce, or motivate the learning of mathematics.

The Instructional System in Mathematics specifies a standard of mastery for each objective so that student progress at different schools and in different classrooms will have essentially the same meaning. The major goal of the program is to help students master elementary and pre-algebra mathematics. At the same time, positive attitudes are fostered. The functional importance of mathematics at home and on the job, in most career opportunities and technological developments, is made clear.

Because ISM is used throughout the Montgomery County Public Schools, the district is reluctant to highlight instances of conspicuous acceleration. Some few students (6–10 in a district serving 93,000 students) have been ready for algebra by grade two or grade three. Many students are ready for algebra by grade five or six. Indeed, Mathematics Coordinator Thomas Rowan reports that the greatest problem in placement is dealing with parental pressure for linear acceleration of students who have not developed a sufficient conceptual base to justify acceleration.

In Claremore, Oklahoma, a similar approach provides continuous progress in mathematics for all fifth-, sixth-, and seventh-grade students at **Walter J. Leeper Middle School.** Students are aged 9 through 13 years; the general program content spans third through eighth grade skill areas.

*The school has developed its own computer
software to facilitate the sorting and placement
of students, by skill levels, with
appropriate teachers.*

The Progressive Mastery Learning math program (PML) was designed as a pure form of outcome-based instruction. At the time of reporting the relatively new program included fifth-, sixth-, and seventh-grade students. Plans were in place to extend the program to encompass first through seventh grades, and expansion into the secondary curriculum was under consideration. Initially, committee members developed the program's scope and sequence of math skills, from fourth through seventh grades, for 60 individual skill levels. The program now encompasses 88 skill areas from third grade through eighth grade. School-wide scheduling was modified to allow all students, most teachers, and some administrators to participate in the math program at the same hour of the day. All students, including gifted, learning disabled, and educable mentally handicapped as well as average students, participate in the program. The school has developed its own computer software to facilitate the sorting and placement of students, by skill levels, with appropriate teachers.

Students entering the program at Leeper are assigned to instructional groups on the basis of placement tests, age, and learning rate. At the initial meeting of a group, the students are tested on content/skill objectives. Mastery (90%) on a pretest allows the student to advance immediately to the next higher skill. In general a math group stays together and is tested over a unit of instruction at the same time. If, however, a student learns more rapidly or more slowly than others in the group, that student will be placed with a more appropriate group.

Teachers at Leeper believe students learn most effectively in groups, with the opportunity to interact with the teacher and with one another. Instruction includes presentations, small and large group discussions, class activities, and guided independent practice of specific skills. When the teacher is confident that a group of students has learned the content of a unit, the teacher gives the end-of-unit test. Those who demonstrate mastery (80% in most skills, 100% in some) move on to the next instructional unit; those who do not receive additional instruction and later demonstrate mastery before moving to the next unit. Each quarter, as a part of the regular report card, parents receive a mathematics skill level report and a graphic representation of their child's progress compared with the appropriate grade-level average.

After the PML program had been in place for one year, the achievement of students in the new program was compared with the achievement of students in a traditional math program, using the SRA achievement test. Fifth-graders in the PML program achieved, on average, .6 of a year more than students in a traditional program; sixth-graders advanced .9 of a year ahead of students in a traditional program. Administrators at Leeper Middle School claim a 54% increase in overall learning as a result of the PML approach. Seventy percent of the students gained more in a year than would be expected using traditional methods; 23% gained about what would be expected; only 7% failed to gain as much in a year as would be expected.

In general, respondents from the schools we surveyed concentrated on the acceleration that results naturally for the most able students. When Mary M. Bray, a curriculum assistant, and Colleen Passaro, a teacher, reported on **Lecanto Primary School** in Citrus County, Florida, they talked about flexible pacing for all 920 students in the school. It is noticeable, however, that the percentage of students at Lecanto Primary who are advanced 1 year or 2 years above grade level is about the same as that at other schools (we will return to this issue in Chapter 7, Selected Features of Flexible Pacing).

At Lecanto Primary School continuous progress is encouraged at all grade levels (K–5) and across all content areas. Individual pacing occurs most widely in reading and mathematics. The organizational structure of the school is informal, open, and consciously innovative. Grades K–5 are arranged in multi-grade pods of four to six classes. Students are heterogeneously assigned to homerooms by grade levels, but this classification is deemphasized. The school uses mastery learning, and each child progresses to the next level when he or she has successfully completed the prerequisites.

Various forms of enrichment complement the continuous progress option at Lecanto. Decisions regarding horizontal or vertical enrichment—expanding on what has been learned or moving to a higher skill level—are based on the developmental or instructional level of the student in each content area, rather than on age or homeroom grade. The staff is trained in teaming, and each teacher is encouraged to develop and share individual talents with the team. Curriculum committees at the school level develop, review, and coordinate the instructional programs. Having a wide variety of materials at different levels available to all has enabled the school to challenge the students at their own levels.

We have illustrated that flexible pacing is often introduced to meet the needs of a special population (usually gifted students) or to accommodate variable learning rates in a particular subject area

*Eliminating the grade levels in language arts
and math/science has improved the students'
sense of achievement.*

(commonly mathematics). The Cedar Hill school district in Texas illustrates another way of introducing flexible pacing, specifically continuous progress, for a limited portion of the student population. A rapidly expanding suburb of Dallas, Cedar Hill is adding one elementary school each year for 3 successive years. The district expects to add five schools in 6 years. In line with its commitment to the Pyramid Project in four Dallas/Fort Worth area school districts (see Chapter 6, Cooperative Programs) and as part of its plan to develop a comprehensive program for able learners, Cedar Hill has elected to introduce continuous progress in the new schools as they open. **High Pointe Elementary** was the first to implement this form of flexible pacing.

As they assigned personnel for the new school, the administration made it clear to staff members and to parents that the new elementary school would use continuous progress in language arts and in math and science (see Appendix B, The High Pointe Plan). The school day is scheduled in three time blocks so that all students are in language arts at the same time, grouped according to achievement level rather than by age. Placement is based on criterion-referenced tests developed by the teachers or provided by the regional educational service center. Similarly, in math and science the students are grouped according to ability, and the grouping in this block is different from the grouping for language arts. In language arts and in the math/science block the students have no sense that they are in a "grade." They study at the level appropriate to their own achievement. In both blocks the students are assessed regularly, and the grouping is adjusted every 5 weeks. For the third block of the elementary curriculum, called humanities, the students are grouped according to age. This is the one block in the curriculum where students are with their age-mates and think of themselves as being in a grade.

At High Pointe Elementary the physical plant has three subject area wings: a language arts wing, a mathematics/science wing, and a humanities wing. Superintendent Joe Neely reports that eliminating the grade levels in language arts and math/science has improved the students' sense of achievement. Students of higher than average ability are allowed to accelerate as their development dictates. For students

---

Any form of flexible pacing struggles against a host of conceptual foes.

---

of lower than average ability, he claims, failure has been eliminated. Standardized testing, using the Iowa Test of Basic Skills, confirms that the placement of students at their achievement levels has been essentially accurate according to national norms.

Because continuous progress is new at High Pointe, the school's experience is limited. Neely counts among the early successes the appropriate placement of students. For example, one 7-year-old student would have been retained in the first grade in the year continuous progress was adopted. Under the new plan the youngster was kept with his age-mates, insofar as he had a grade assignment, but he received instruction in language and in math and science at a level he could comprehend, and without the stigma of failing a year in school. Another student, who enrolled in kindergarten already able to read, was placed with a class reading at second-grade level and made remarkable progress.

The **Ardmore** (Oklahoma) **City Schools** have been affiliated with the Pyramid Project schools in Texas. Also committed to the flexible pacing approach central to that project, the Ardmore schools began by introducing continuous progress throughout the school district first in mathematics (fall, 1985), the following year in language arts, and then in social sciences. In consultation with the Gifted Students Institute and working with a curriculum sequence developed by Ardmore teachers, the district grouped all students according to their scores on a district criterion test, an achievement test, prior classroom performance, and teacher recommendations. Kindergarten students are grouped all together for the first semester, then across class and grade boundaries in the second semester. Students in grades 1–8 are grouped according to achievement level and performance. In grades 1–5 each elementary school follows a class schedule workable for its own building. Nearly all schools schedule a single mathematics block; the size of the school and other local differences determine the scheduling that works best for language arts and social sciences.

Although flexible pacing is new in Ardmore, the district is beginning to develop anecdotal evidence of its success. Director of instruction Deanne Broughton, reporting for the district, writes of a fifth-grader named Sarah, who after 2 years of progressing at her own pace was completing seventh grade mathematics objectives. The story is familiar: Sarah is shown a math concept once and is allowed time to practice on her own. Her practice time may be no more than 10 minutes. When she is ready, she asks to be tested over the objective she has learned. Sarah was expected to be ready for algebra by the time she entered sixth grade.

SUMMARY

We have been careful to distinguish *flexible pacing,* a more comprehensive term, from *continuous progress,* one specific manifestation of it. All the elementary schools we have covered use some version of continuous progress. It is the option of choice in these schools, the instructional arrangement they strive to achieve.

Two important threads run through this account of flexible pacing at the elementary level. The first is that continuous progress is frequently introduced gradually, with a carefully selected student population. Within the recent history of continuous progress—as opposed to the longer history of ability grouping—able learners, often the gifted and talented, have been targeted for continuous progress on a school-wide or district-wide scale. Some districts have selected a single subject area, usually mathematics, as a starting place for developing a curriculum sequence upon which to mount continuous progress. In some instances it has proved logistically feasible to introduce this form of flexible pacing at a single school for students of all abilities in all the major subject areas.

This pattern of introducing continuous progress one step at a time is not essential, but it reflects the feeling among school administrators and curriculum specialists that continuous progress must earn acceptance in a predominantly conservative setting. Any form of flexible pacing struggles against a host of conceptual foes: the egalitarian view of education that sees standardized treatment as the only vehicle of equality; the awareness that mastery learning requires a rethinking, often a disruption, of timeworn methods of classroom management; the recognition that flexible pacing will inevitably result in dispersion of students of diverse abilities along a continuum of achievement levels that cannot be easily separated into grade levels. Continuous progress, if it succeeds, looks messy.

And over all these reasons for reluctance floats the spectre of social adjustment, the unfounded belief that youngsters between the ages of 5 and 13 can mature naturally only among classmates of just the same age. The resistance is discouraging; a school or district must move with caution.

*Our ability has provided management
capabilities that make continuous progress and
other forms of flexible pacing possible.*

The second thread that runs through these anecdotal accounts of flexible pacing is more optimistic. Written into every response we received from a school identified as practicing flexible pacing in one form or another is the enthusiasm of pioneers, explorers if you will, aware that they are engaged in an exciting experiment. While flexible pacing is in one sense an old idea, a return to a form of instruction that predates modern urbanized education, it is relatively new in school districts that number their student populations in the thousands. To a large extent, what might be called a revolutionary idea in education is the fulfillment of Alvin Toffler's prediction of a "breakdown of the factory-model school" (1971, p. 407). The fifth trend of John Naisbitt's "Megatrends" is from centralization to decentralization, from homogeneity to diversity (1984, pp. 103–141). Naisbitt claims that with computer technology a company can have a distinct and individually tailored arrangement with each of thousands of employees (1984, p. 89). Our ability to store, recall, and process information and to reproduce records has provided management capabilities that make continuous progress and other forms of flexible pacing possible in schools and districts where the sheer numbers would have been forbidding a few years ago.

Typically, teachers, administrators, and parents of children in schools with flexible pacing are excited by the progress they see among their children. The practice is still too new to have massive statistical support. The evidence with which we have worked is subjective and of short duration. It is, however, persuasive. The most obvious effect reported by the schools we heard from is that the highly able learners, no longer held back by lockstep advancement, are able to surge ahead in their basic skills and in the learning they acquire. But all youngsters appear to benefit from the shift to continuous progress. Slow learners, according to our reports, are able to move at a comfortable pace without the threat of failure. The predictable result some respondents feared, that the slow students would become lazy with the pressure off, has not materialized. And the large middle group, treated statistically as normal, has benefited as well. Because of the individualizing entailed by continuous progress, more nearly average students receive the same personal attention as the very able or the very slow. As a consequence, their learning abilities thrive.

CHAPTER 4

Flexible Pacing at the Secondary Level

Our description of flexible pacing in elementary schools makes it clear that the mixture of instructional strategies and the shifting of students can be untidy. As students are grouped and regrouped, moved from class to class, shuttled between grades, even transported from campus to campus, the image of the traditional schoolroom with neat rows and children sitting quietly at their desks, dissolves and is replaced with one of fluid motion, constant rearrangement—in short, a picture of life.

The scene at a high school during the transition between class periods dramatizes what happens when students are grouped for instruction according to the logic of the curriculum rather than that of age grading. When the bell rings, the doors to the individual classrooms burst open, and the halls become a circulatory system. Students who have been grouped in one way for a given period of instruction flow through the halls in apparently random fashion for several minutes, then regroup themselves for the next instructional period. It looks chaotic, but it makes sense.

But in the typical high school, where students move from room to room between classes, looks can be deceiving. Whether the classes to which the students move are flexible in the pacing of the curriculum and whether students are allowed to shift from class to class as they master skills and content cannot be determined from the simple motion of bodies. It may be true, for example, that all students graduating from a single high school, or from all high schools in a single district, have exactly the same number of credits, in the same courses offered in a prescribed order, taken in just the same number of years.

By our definition flexible pacing allows students to progress through the curriculum at variable rates, determined primarily by their performance. The common ways of achieving flexible pacing in secondary school include allowing the students to shift between grade levels, and varying the rate and content of instruction in individual classes. When highly able students are allowed to transfer from grade to grade among classes, the consequence is frequently early entrance to the next institutional level or concurrent enrollment in more than one level. Thus in a flexible system students younger than high school age may attend the high school for part or all of the day. Those who have completed the normal high school sequences may attend a nearby college for some of their coursework, or they may graduate ahead of schedule.

In an earlier treatment of options for able learners (Cox, Daniel, & Boston, 1985), we devoted considerable attention to the **Bishop Carroll High School**, in Calgary, Alberta, which uses continuous progress at the secondary level to achieve flexible pacing throughout its curriculum. At Bishop Carroll each student follows a personal performance schedule that includes independent study and group sessions, planned with and approved by a teacher/advisor. The group sessions are not required, but the students find them useful in completing the requirements in each subject area. To clarify the Bishop Carroll requirements, we include a paragraph from our earlier study:

> To graduate, students must meet requirements in nine subject areas: English language arts, fine arts, health fitness and recreation, mathematics, modern languages, philosophy and religious studies, practical arts, science, and social studies. Each course in these subject areas carries five credits toward graduation and is divided into units of work through which the students move at their own pace. While a minimum of 100 credits is required for graduation, the students at Bishop Carroll normally exceed that number. In general, students at Bishop Carroll High School complete 115–120 credits in about three years (Cox, Daniel, & Boston, 1985, p. 139).

We have been unable to locate a school in the United States with a similarly flexible approach. A school or district that chose to adopt the Bishop Carroll system would have to rethink the whole method of assigning high school credits. The most widely accepted and institutionalized way of varying the rate and content of instruction for superior students is by offering Advanced Placement courses (AP) (Gallagher, 1985b). Another common option for able learners is courses based on the curriculum of the International Baccalaureate (IB) (Fox, 1985).

AP and IB courses are designed for superior students in the 11th and 12th grades (AP examinations may be taken by students as early as 10th grade). While specific content in the AP courses is determined locally, broad outlines of the content to be covered in each course and

> *The most widely accepted and institutionalized*
> *way of varying the rate and content of*
> *instruction for superior students is by*
> *offering Advanced Placement courses.*

information on the methods of examination are provided by the College Entrance Examination Board. The courses culminate in examinations conducted by the Educational Testing Service in Princeton, the nearest thing to national examinations offered in this country. Similarly, the International Baccalaureate, conceived as a total curriculum rather than as separate courses, is governed by an external agency, the International Baccalaureate Office in Geneva. The examinations, administered locally, are read by an international board of examiners.

The Talent Identification Program, Duke University, recently published a series of AP teacher's manuals, designed to assist local educators as they prepare AP or other rigorous courses. Materials include more depth and scope than previously available. For information, contact The Talent Identification Program, Duke University, Box 40077, Durham, NC 27706–0077.

Neither AP courses nor the IB curriculum leads to early graduation from high school. Indeed, both AP and IB coursework are motivated in part by the institution's desire to keep the better students in high school for their junior and senior years even though some of these students might easily complete the regular curriculum 1 or 2 years early and so qualify for early graduation and admission to college.

Advanced Placement courses and the International Baccalaureate qualify as flexible pacing, by our definition, in two ways. One is that both options offer advanced coursework, essentially at college level, before the students leave the high school campus. Students who successfully complete either individual courses, designated as AP courses for example, or the complete curriculum of the International Baccalaureate, typically qualify for advanced standing upon admission to college or university. Although no uniform policy guides admission at receiving colleges, a score of 3 or better on an AP examination usually enables the student to receive credit on the college transcript or placement in an advanced course in the discipline. Many colleges treat satisfactory scores on IB examination as the equivalent of AP credit, and some will grant sophomore status to a student who successfully completes the IB diploma. Thus, without leaving the high school campus these students have already begun higher education and have earned credits that will transfer to their college transcripts.

The other way AP and IB offerings fit our definition of flexible pacing is that both entail early preparation at an advanced level. For example, to enroll in AP calculus in the junior or senior year, a student must have completed the entire pre-calculus curriculum. Normally the student will have been accelerated through the math sequence, starting as early as the fifth or sixth grade. In foreign language, particularly important to the IB diploma, a student must have mastered a foreign language beyond the level usually achieved in an American high school. To reach that level of language proficiency, the student must normally begin to study the language early, again about fifth or sixth grade, before foreign language study is offered in most of our school systems. Similar accelerated preparation is required by the IB curriculum in such areas as English, social studies, and natural sciences.

To gather information for this section of our study we tried to identify schools with strong offerings in Advanced Placement or those that offer the International Baccalaureate. The Southwest regional office of the College Board provided a list of about 100 schools with strong AP offerings in a wide range of subjects. The office of International Baccalaureate North America provided a similar list of IB schools with a record of success. To broaden our survey we also used the list of schools who had won National High School Recognition Awards for 1986–1987, given by the United States Department of Education. To each of the schools identified in this way we sent a questionnaire. What we have to say about flexible pacing at the secondary level is based on the questionnaires that were returned.

Our presentation is weighted toward schools offering AP coursework. The imbalance reflects the difference in emphasis at U. S. high schools between the College Board's AP program, well-established nationwide, and the relatively new IB program. While the number of schools offering AP coursework is in the thousands, in January, 1987, 114 American schools offered coursework toward the International Baccalaureate.

THE ADVANCED PLACEMENT OPTION

Haverford Senior High School in Havertown, Pennsylvania, provides five options for enriched or accelerated learning which their superior students can choose from or combine. In addition to a full range of AP courses (in American history, biology, chemistry, computer science, English, European history, French language, mathematics, and physics), the high school offers concurrent enrollment at middle school

---

The school views accelerated and honors academic work not as a prize for past work, but as a challenge and a commitment.

---

and high school and concurrent enrollment at the high school and nearby colleges and universities. Haverford High has an array of honors courses in subjects for 9th through 11th grade that prepare students for AP courses. In addition there are opportunities for independent study that we have not treated as flexible pacing options.

Two features of the Haverford High program deserve special notice. The first is the Haverford policy of self-selection. If a student, the student's parents, or a school counselor feels the student has the ability to work at a high level, and particularly if the student wants to, the youngster is encouraged to sign up for any of the advanced programs. Students do not take entrance exams or qualify by high grades or the recommendations of their previous teachers. The school views accelerated and honors academic work not as a prize for past work, but as a challenge and a commitment. If a student finds the work extremely difficult or if the student is overcommitted in time, the student may, during the first part of the academic year, drop back to a less intensive course with no penalties or stigma.

To illustrate this feature of their program, Dean of Academic Programs Richard Tyre refers to a two-period-per-day honors humanities seminar taught by two former college professors using college materials and standards. Because it has no formal prerequisites, the course attracts, and the school officially encourages, students who have never taken an AP or honors course to elect it if they wish. Of approximately 65 seniors who take the course each year, usually about 10 are students who have never taken an honors course. According to Tyre, two or three of these students each year show themselves to be as bright as the state-designated "gifted students." Five or six earn Bs or Cs but may learn as much as their more gifted peers.

The other feature of the Haverford High School program worth noticing, even though it is not unique, is the considerable ease with which students can cross the boundaries between institutional levels to get instruction suited to their learning levels. Because the middle school is adjacent to the senior high school, the district encourages able middle school students to walk to the high school for courses when their achievement warrants such a move. This option is exercised most often in mathematics and foreign languages. In a normal year not more than about 10 students require this flexible option. There are almost always one or two students accelerated 2 or 3 years ahead of their normal grade placement in perhaps one subject. If enough accelerated students need coursework in a single subject, the district selects and trains a teacher to give the course at the high school level on the middle school campus. The counseling departments of the middle school and the high school are experienced in creating special schedules so that students can take advantage of concurrent enrollment without missing other academic, social, or extracurricular experiences in their home school.

In addition, Haverford High School is less than 2 miles from Haverford College and Bryn Mawr College and within easy traveling distance of Villanova University, St. Joseph's, the University of Pennsylvania, and Temple University. Because the high school offers some 20 AP or honors courses, the school feels no pressure to encourage their able students to attend local colleges and universities while still in high school. On the other hand, advanced seniors occasionally need a course only given at one of these institutions. The district has a special arrangement with Villanova University that allows one or two seniors each year to take a necessary course at the university, tuition free. The school has one or two juniors each year, self-selected, who skip their senior year or leave after the first semester of their senior year and go straight to college.

In addition to these more formal options, Haverford High School allows students to test out of courses with full credit under any of the following conditions: they have studied the subject at a foreign school or a university; they have taken a semester or a year abroad; they have done specialized work outside the school; they have been tutored at home.

The self-selection policy of Haverford High School is designed to provide ample opportunity for enrichment and advancement to all students. A different approach to this challenge characterizes the advanced curriculum at Walnut Hills High School in Cincinnati, Ohio. Entrance to the school is competitive and based in part on an admissions test and academic performance. Once in, the students are screened for the advanced education program. At the seventh grade all students enter a foundation program of required courses, including Latin. Based on algebra readiness testing and previous mathematics achievement, 5–10% of the class is accelerated into an algebra program to start a sequence that will lead through AP calculus to a calculus-based probability and statistics course for seniors, the equivalent of four to five semesters of college-level mathematics while in high school. For all other classes, seventh-graders from over 80 elementary schools are mixed in a program with a common beginning.

At grades 8 and 9 the top 25% of the class is invited into a 2-year interdisciplinary honors program. The team-taught honors program links three related subjects scheduled as a block for half the school day. For example, the ninth-grade theme is the classical heritage, and students study Latin, ancient and medieval history, and English. During the third quarter, they learn about the Roman empire in history, read Shakespeare's *Julius Caesar* in English, and translate Caesar's *Gaullic Campaigns* from Latin.

At grade 10 the advanced curriculum expands to include advanced academic (AA) and Advanced Placement (AP) courses. The AA courses, offered in English, Mathematics, and Modern Foreign Languages, prepare students to enter college-level AP work. At grade 10 over 40% of Walnut Hills students are involved in the advanced curriculum. AP courses are available to 10th graders in Latin, Art History, and Music Appreciation.

In grades 11 and 12 the AA courses continue and more AP courses are added. Walnut Hills offers one of the larger AP programs in the nation; in 1987, 350 students took 595 AP exams in 20 subjects. By graduation about half of each senior class has participated in the advanced curriculum. Approximately 18% of each senior class qualifies for potential sophomore status in college by performing successfully on AP examinations in three or more disciplines.

Walnut Hills High School represents its advanced academic curriculum as an inverted pyramid to reflect the higher number of courses and the increased level of student participation in the higher grades (see Table 1).

Acceptance to honors, AA, and AP courses is based on three criteria: student grades (3.5 in the specific subject, 3.0 overall), teacher recommendations, and high tested achievement (CAT stanines of 8 or 9, PSAT over 48). While in the courses students must maintain a B average on a special scale that holds C as unsatisfactory. Students who earn two Cs in a subject are withdrawn from the advanced curriculum and placed in the normal college preparatory level of the course.

Critics of the advanced curriculum at Walnut Hills contend that it leads to a two-track system, stripping student leadership from the normal college preparatory program. Racial clustering is likely, they say, and the press for achievement is sometimes too intense in advanced classes. The school's response to these charges is to work continually for increased participation in the advanced curriculum and to keep the boundary between the two levels as fluid as possible. Academic counseling and support in developing advanced study skills and improved time management are offered to students. According to Assistant Principal Ward Ghory, an interest group of parents, teachers, and students supports the advanced curriculum, keeping attention focused on the staff development need implied by providing

TABLE 1

Walnut Hills High School Advanced Academic Curriculum

Grade			*Percentage of Students Involved*
12	Advanced	Placement	Courses (16)	48
11	Advanced Academic (7)	Advanced Placement (11)	48
10	Adv. Academic (8)	Adv. Placement (3)	46
9	Honors, Advanced Academic (4)		24
8	Honors (8)		22
7	Algebra (7)		8

(The number of courses offered at each level is shown in parentheses)

flexible pacing and accelerated content for a diverse group of students within the single classroom.

In contrast to Haverford High School and Walnut Hills High School, which emphasize self-selection and modest entrance requirements, **Whitney High School**, in Cerritos, California, is an alternative school for academically motivated students, a public but more selective university preparatory magnet school. Students qualify for admission on the basis of high test scores (School and College Ability Test III), good grades, and teacher recommendations. Because of the stringent entrance requirements, Whitney students automatically qualify for most of the accelerated classes and other special programs.

Programs we would count as flexible pacing include Advanced Placement courses, other honors courses, and concurrent enrollment in high school and college. The AP program at Whitney High has grown from 2 classes and 30 students in 1982 to 15 classes at eight levels in five subject areas, serving about 300 students. In the coming year two more subject areas will be added. Acceleration is encouraged in several subject areas and is fairly widespread in mathematics and foreign language.

Whitney High School keeps careful records of its students' college admissions as one way of assessing the program. The school devotes extraordinary attention to individual analysis and counseling in the matter of college and university placement and scholarship assistance. The school claims a stable 95% acceptance to 4-year universities. In addition, the school has scored in the 99th percentile in all areas on the California Assessment Program (CAP). Recent awards for the high

*The College Aspiration Partnership Program,
provides special assistance to ensure adequate
college preparation for underrepresented
minority and disadvantaged students.*

school include recognition as one of California's distinguished high schools (among the top 30 high schools in the state) and a U.S. Department of Education National Recognition Award.

Among the assets that account for Whitney High School's high level of success are a faculty and administration that reach for new instructional strategies and programming opportunities. The principal, a counselor, and a teacher are members of the University of California Academic Fellows program, which meets monthly at Irvine to generate methods and programs to meet the special needs of college-bound students. Six members of the faculty are involved in a mentoring program that encourages unique projects for students. Whitney participates in the College Aspiration Partnership Program, which provides special assistance to ensure adequate college preparation for underrepresented minority and disadvantaged students. The school points with pride to the achievement that in 1986 100% of Whitney's underrepresented minority students were accepted by 4-year universities.

The Whitney High School experience illustrates that flexible pacing contributes to and depends on a kind of outreach that extends the view of students and faculty beyond the insular community of the high school. Students and faculty share the conviction that high school is not the end of education but the launching ground for higher education. To translate this conviction into realistic and productive curriculum and instruction requires that high school teachers and administrators work closely with their professional colleagues at the university level.

In Mobile, Alabama, **Murphy High School** demonstrates what can be accomplished in an inner-city school by applying a systematic honors/AP approach with a nonselective, heterogeneous urban population. An older school with a proud history, Murphy High School achieved some recognition in the 1950s for its core curriculum, a model educational plan featured in at least one textbook on high school curriculum (mentioned by Principal Paul J. Sousa in his personal communication, 1987). In the 1960s and early 1970s, as a result of the Mobile integration plan and resulting white flight, the school experienced changes in tone and educational focus and a loss of support from the community. Accepting these changes as a challenge, the school has clung to its strong academic tradition. In the late 1970s the school introduced AP courses to meet the special needs of their better students and to upgrade the curriculum.

The school began with English, using one teacher in one course. By 1982 Murphy High School had 78 students taking AP exams, and in 1986, Paul Sousa reports, the school gave 235 AP exams in 12 different AP courses. Early in the development of their program Murphy High School formed an honors/AP department made up of all 9th- through 12th-grade teachers of honors classes. Coordinating the honors and AP classes to provide continuity in each discipline, the department also worked to correlate course materials across disciplines. For example, one year the honors government and AP English teachers presented an anti-utopian unit using Skinner's *Walden II* and Golding's *Lord of the Flies*. The next semester the honors economics teacher presented a unit on the Great Depression while the AP English classes were reading Steinbeck's *Grapes of Wrath*.

To raise awareness among the faculty and to provide help in handling the challenges of an advanced curriculum, Murphy High School has been active in the national AP movement, sending delegates to the national and regional College Board conferences. The head of the Honors/AP department is a reader for the national College Board English examinations. Murphy High School sends teachers to local, regional, and national workshops for training during the summer months.

Among the benefits to the school and its students of having an active honors/AP program are increased community awareness, solid support from parents, and important recognition for the students. The senior class of 1982 produced six National Merit Finalists. In 1987 Murphy was selected as a model school in the U. S. Department of Education's Secondary School Recognition Program. We notice that the impact of Murphy High School's flexible pacing option and corollary curricular adjustments goes beyond simply garnering college credits for selected students. It results in an improved educational atmosphere school-wide.

A similar concentration on the Advanced Placement option for able learners at the high school level characterizes the program at **Middletown High School**, in Middletown, Maryland. A program started in 1982–1983, in which 13 students took AP exams in four subjects, grew in 3 years to one in which the senior class of 1986, although the same total size as the 1983 class, took 112 tests in 13 areas. Plans to expand the offerings the following year indicate that the AP program is still growing.

One of the principal arguments for offering AP coursework suggests that the exams themselves, and the college credit for which students

*The nationally administered AP exams exert
a form of control, a guarantee that the level of
instruction will be sufficient to prepare students
to perform as well as their abilities should allow.*

may qualify by taking them, are a minor benefit of the AP course. More important justifications for the increased rigor of the courses, the advanced content level, and the more demanding pace are, first, that such improved courses offer a more suitable challenge to the learning abilities of the students and, second, that a spin-off effect alters the expectations of all students and teachers in all courses. This is especially true of those courses preliminary to the AP courses, those that prepare the students to do college-level work before they leave high school.

At the same time, the nationally administered AP exams exert a form of control, a guarantee that the level of instruction will be sufficient to prepare students to perform as well as their abilities should allow. Whether a high school requires or recommends that its students accept the challenge and sit for the exams is therefore a matter of some consequence. The Middletown High School and its school board feel it would be improper to force all students in an AP course to take the examination. Yet they don't want students to shy away from the challenge of rigorous testing. They therefore offer two options: students may either take the College Board exams or they may substitute a 3-hour Middletown test—usually a College Board exam from an earlier year. Most of the students take the College Board test and a high percentage earn college credit.

Another flexible pacing option available to Middletown High School students is an administrative waiver of full-day enrollment in order to take classes at Frederick Community College. Students are released from one period at Middletown High for every class they take at the community college; they are also granted one additional released period for travel. Courses taken at the community college must complement, not replace, courses available at the high school. This option, a version of flexible pacing because it advances students to postsecondary learning, is typically chosen by students from the enriched and on-grade tracks of Middletown's high school population rather than by those who elect the AP options.

The presence of a tracking system at Middletown High School, which in fact begins in sixth grade, suggests that students may have their secondary and postsecondary options determined for them at an early age. The district and the high school have devoted considerable attention to this possibility, and they do their best to encourage students to participate in the more challenging academic programs. As a matter of policy, any student may participate in accelerated classes, and no program is closed to any student.

A program similar to the administrative waiver option available in the Maryland high school is provided by Minnesota's Post Secondary Enrollment Options Act. Under this act any student may apply to study at a college or university of the student's choice. The cost of this educational option, including books and tuition, is the responsibility of the state. Students provide their own transportation. The college work may be used for either high school credit or college credit, not both.

Centennial High School, in Circle Pines, Minnesota, reports that many of its students take advantage of the Post Secondary Enrollment Option. Because most of the students who choose this option are ahead of schedule in earning high school credits, most do not need the high school credit. The students are banking credits on a college transcript, and this option is therefore a form of flexible pacing even if the students are taking courses in vocational or practical rather than academic subject areas. Centennial High School also offers AP courses in a limited number of subjects, and students are encouraged to take the examinations in order to earn college credits.

In reporting on its flexible pacing options, **Valley High School,** in Sacramento, California, describes both concurrent enrollment in high school and college and Advanced Placement offerings. The concurrent enrollment option is like those of Maryland and Minnesota in being required by the state. In California concurrent enrollment is available to all certified gifted and talented students in grades 9–12, and to all 11th- and 12th-grade students with an average of B or better. According to Administrative Assistant Richard Morris, reporting for Valley High School, the proximity of a community college and a state university makes concurrent enrollment easy and reduces the demand for a wide array of AP courses. The success of the concurrent enrollment program depends primarily on coordinating advising and guidance between the schools at both levels and on interinstitutional articulation. Formal articulation conferences involving staff members from community colleges and high schools are held several times each year. Several university outreach programs provide early college orientation programs and ease the transition from high school to college.

At Valley High School it is possible to complete up to a year of college prior to graduation, through accelerated coursework leading to Advanced Placement classes or concurrent enrollment in college classes or both. The emphasis of the Valley High School program is on early preparation in the principal subjects of English, mathematics, science, and social science.

Valley High School provides advanced classes for 9th- and 10th-grade students in the four principal areas. The math courses are the same courses that are offered to students in the upper grade levels. Students are given accelerated placement at the junior high level. In English and social sciences special courses have been designed for academically talented students, and these courses stress literature and writing. Science courses are college preparatory classes with laboratory activities.

Conscious and continuing program articulation is regarded as an important part of staff development. Instructors meet regularly to articulate goals and objectives both between disciplines and throughout the levels. Regular Advanced Placement seminars and inservice training on exemplary teaching practices in the several disciplines contribute to the success of the program.

THE INTERNATIONAL BACCALAUREATE OPTION

Attention to staff development offers an occasion to conclude our survey of secondary schools offering AP and shift our focus to the IB option at **Chandler High School** in Chandler, Arizona. Chandler High School has an articulation agreement with Mesa Community College for certain vocational (business and technical) courses that allows the students in their high school courses to master the objectives of the corresponding community college courses and receive college credit for the work. Although these courses are not typically taken by academically talented students, they do offer students the opportunity to get into college-level work before they graduate from high school.

Chandler High School also has three higher-level academic programs designed to challenge the students and ensure superior preparation for college. The honors course program offers classes qualitatively different from courses in the regular curriculum, intended to provide additional challenge and honor grade points but no college credit. By our definition these courses, in seven academic areas, should not be called flexible pacing, for they do not lead to college credit. They are part of an integrated program, however, and honors courses at the lower levels prepare students to enter AP and IB coursework.

The other higher-level programs are those we are focusing on, Advanced Placement and the International Baccalaureate. Chandler High School has a considerable investment in its AP and IB offerings. Each year the school sends a number of teachers to subject-matter conferences to increase their understanding of the demands of these courses that culminate in external examinations. The faculty members learn about content and also about methods of instruction. Reports on the results of the testing suggest that the money is well spent.

To illustrate, in the summer of 1985, Chandler High sent five teachers to a subject-matter conference in Dallas, and, in the summer of 1986, five to a similar conference in Vancouver. The number of students involved in AP and IB coursework has remained fairly constant (60 students in 1985/86, 61 students in 1986/87). Assistant Principal Harold Dusick reports that in credits earned through AP testing, the 1987 results show a 24% increase over those of 1986 and a 70% increase over those of 1985. While it is impossible to establish a direct correlation or infer a cause for the improved performance, it is fair to say that the Chandler High School has shown an improvement in the measurable results of its AP and IB courses.

Rufus King High School for the College Bound, in Milwaukee, Wisconsin, is a city-wide magnet school whose mission is to provide a rigorous academic curriculum for students with an expressed desire to successfully complete college. One of three Wisconsin high schools authorized to offer the International Baccalaureate curriculum, King High School has been an IB school since 1980. At the time of reporting (figures through 1987) 29 full International Baccalaureate diplomas had been awarded to King students, and 1,020 certificates had been granted for successful completion of IB examinations.

King High School is urban, its student population ethnically diverse. Of 1,192 students, 629 are listed by ethnic code as Black, 495 as White, and the remaining students as Asian, Spanish, American Indian, or other. A profile of International Baccalaureate diploma holders lists the colleges at which these students have matriculated: University of Wisconsin-Madison, University of California-Berkeley, Harvard, Yale, Brown, Amherst, and others, totaling some 13 separate institutions.

The student population at King is self-selected. Participation in the IB program is voluntary but requires successful completion of pre-IB courses in English, biology, mathematics, and chemistry. The IB diploma demands 3 years of a modern foreign language and 3 years of mathematics, as well as the IB's Theory of Knowledge course and its cultural aesthetic and social service requirement. The program itself ensures that the students are highly motivated able learners.

A mimeographed publication, "What Keeps King So Special" (1988), highlights the achievements of present and former students, including scholarships in art, prizes in writing contests, participation in foreign exchange programs, and active involvement in a wide range of enrichment activities. Students from King High School have performed creditably in state and national academic competitions and have received scholarships to participate in scientific expeditions through-out the world. While no figures are available to indicate college credits earned in high school and no uniform policy determines how receiving

---

*The IB curriculum allows any district to provide
the necessary international emphasis while it
meets the regular state guidelines.*

---

colleges place students with IB diplomas, it is safe to say that these students start their college careers with an advantage over students who have not been accelerated in their high school years.

The International Baccalaureate has burgeoned in the last 10 years as an option for increasing the challenge for able learners in the state schools of many nations. The growth of IB schools in North America has been on the order of 20% per year (Fox, 1985). While the IB got its start in this country in cities with international populations—at the United Nations School in New York, the International School in Washington, D.C.—the IB curriculum allows any district to provide the necessary international emphasis while it meets the regular state guidelines. The list of IB schools includes high schools in Harlingen, Texas, Southfield, Michigan, and other communities away from major cities. Of the students taking the IB in the United States and Canada, 84% are in public school systems (Fox, 1985, p. 64).

When we reported on the International Baccalaureate in the Richardson Study (Cox, Daniel, & Boston, 1985), we looked in particular at what was required of a school district and the teachers in the system to gear up for the increased challenge. The example we used was in Houston, where the IB was inaugurated at **Bellaire High School** in 1980. The Houston Independent School District invested a great deal in the project. To be a member of the IBO costs the participating school annual subscription fees that can run as high as $13,000. An additional fee is required for every student who sits for the examinations. Gathering materials and paying for time spent in curriculum revision and staff development cost the Houston district over $100,000. To prepare for the IB the teachers devoted more than a year to study and self-development. In addition to tightening their courses and adding the material covered on IB examinations, the teachers had to manage their curriculum so as to meet the guidelines of the state education agency. In developing the Theory of Knowledge course and reshaping courses in the social sciences to meet the international requirement, they had to master entirely new material. The effort brought the teachers together in a common purpose and engaged the parents of students being considered for the IB. It meant extra work for all—students, parents, and teachers. But all seemed eager to accept the challenge. The compensation was a heightened sense of mission and a solid dose of self-respect.

Our sampling of schools illustrates that many students can go beyond the limits of the normal high school curriculum and advance well into college work before they leave high school. The opportunity is not bought at the expense of a shortened adolescence, isolation from peers of the same age, or prohibitive personal or family expenses. These options are widespread, institutional, and relatively easy for our school systems to accommodate. The most compelling reason for their existence is that they allow students to encounter a challenging curriculum at every level with a minimum of dislocation. Flexible pacing provides that challenge for students of all abilities at every level of their schooling.

CHAPTER 5

Flexible Pacing at All Levels

To illustrate flexible pacing district-wide at all levels we have descriptions of six school districts. The materials these districts have provided allow us to highlight special features of each district's policies or practices. We have not given a full picture of any district. The overall picture, we hope, will be balanced and will represent accurately the diverse ways flexible pacing is administered, the various forms it can assume, and the enriched experience it offers.

JEFFERSON COUNTY PUBLIC SCHOOLS

The **Jefferson County Public Schools** in central Colorado serve nearly 76,000 students in 114 schools. In line with a Board of Education policy of some 15 years' duration, continuous progress is a district-wide practice. About 25% of the more able learners have been allowed to move ahead of their grade level in one or more subject areas. In addition, the separate schools have their own school-based programs for the gifted and talented, serving approximately 2% of the students.

The Board of Education policy that governs flexible pacing requires that "instructional programs will contain a continuum of learner objectives which will permit continuous learner progress and ensure continuity of learning for each student" (policy submitted by Jefferson County Public Schools). Decisions concerning the placement and progress of students are based on classroom teachers' recommendations and require parents' participation. Continuous progress is the practice in every subject area; a student may be advanced to whatever level provides appropriate challenge in a given discipline.

---

*School-based programming allows each building
to capitalize on the special strengths and
interests of personnel in the individual schools.*

Placement ahead of the normal grade for a given age can occur by grade skipping, as when a third-grade child is advanced directly to fifth grade. If it seems more appropriate, advanced material can be brought down to a student who remains in the same grade with age-mates. At the high school level, College Board Advanced Placement courses and other honors courses are available in a wide variety of subjects.

In its programming for highly able learners, the gifted and talented, the Jefferson County philosophy is that no single program or option will work. District policy encourages "the design and orchestration of many options and alternatives, varying in kind and degree, for individual students with diverse interests and gifts." The best administrative design, in the district's judgment, is a school-based model. "Each school is an individual culture and . . . profound change takes place at the level of that unique culture" (Jefferson County Rationale). School-based programming allows each building to capitalize on the special strengths and interests of personnel in the individual schools.

The policy statement describing options for the gifted student helps us to see how programming for the gifted intersects with and branches out from the basic programs in each of the content areas. The statement outlines options in language arts and reading, library media, mathematics, music, outdoor education, physical education, science, second language, social studies, student guidance services, vocational/ technical education, and school-wide extracurricular activities. To illustrate the programming with a single subject area, we have drawn on the description of the language arts program provided by the district.

The language arts/reading curriculum of the Jefferson County schools has five focus areas, K–12: composition, literature, language study, oral communication, and reading. Each of these strands has an outline of sequential skills and concepts that enable the students to meet their own needs as well as those of the society. Grade-level expectations in each of the five strands are indicated for the "on-target" (average) student in the curriculum guides and student records as well as in the junior and senior high school course guides and the individual skills folders. The continuous nature of the skills sequence in each area allows students to progress according to their separate achievement and ability levels.

The core of each strand, the district claims, is as important to both the high achiever and the gifted student as it is to the underachiever or the student with limited intellectual capacity. While some other academic areas may require adding or deleting topics and activities to meet the needs of students at all ability levels, language arts lends itself to contracting essential elements or to expanding them and exploring "the vast world" of literature, language study, performing arts, and writing.

Students at the elementary level can be targeted to remedy deficiencies through alternative strategies as well as to expand on strengths through the wealth of activities in writing, speaking and listening, studying the language, and exploring literature. At junior high level, the range of literature accommodates all abilities, and the composition units allow either cursory exploration of writing skills or relatively deep study for the high achiever or the gifted student.

At the high school level, clearly discernible differences separate pursuits for students of limited ability, for those "on target," and for high achievers and gifted students. The district feels it is important to identify each student accurately, for the truly gifted student who might flourish in creative writing might wither under the tight structure and expectations of honors or Advanced Placement English. The Jefferson County policy statement points out that while acting and theater production and directing may accommodate a wide range of abilities, it can be a profoundly rewarding experience for the verbally and dramatically gifted student. The rigors of competitive debate, with its demand for meticulous research, may be rewarding to some high achievers yet fail to engage more creative gifted students.

Fundamental to the Jefferson County philosophy is the belief that simple acceleration is not the solution to challenging able learners. In describing the language arts/reading options, the district document urges that communications skills be integrated for all students, especially for gifted students. Pointing out that enrichment in language arts is more appropriate than radical acceleration in reading, the district urges teachers to guide students in the selection of print materials that allow a student to apply writing skills in reacting to literature and to other content. They add that emphasis should be given to development and application of research skills, to opportunities to pursue independent projects over time, to use of higher level questioning, to individual work with mentors, to involvement with the Great Books Program, and to a guided study of literary genres.

NORTH OLMSTED CITY SCHOOLS

Another school district with a firm board of education commitment to continuous progress is the North Olmsted (Ohio) City Schools. The published educational philosophy commits the district to humaneness, continuous progress, and meeting individual needs. Adopted in April, 1985, the policy spells out the commitment as follows:

I. Humaneness provides:
   A. that each student shall have the opportunity to succeed. All those participating in the educational process have the responsibility of providing the kind of environment that promotes success.
   B. that each student shall have the opportunity to develop a positive self-concept and an awareness and concern for the dignity of others.
   C. that each student develop an attitude of responsibility for positive contributions to society.

II. Continuous progress should:
   A. provide a sequence for learning that allows for progress based upon a person's ability and achievement.
   B. recognize that students vary in their interests and capabilities and thus the educational program must provide for these differences.
   C. involve a variety of teaching techniques and interaction with different staff members in order to meet the varied needs of students.
   D. make possible the movement of a student from one instructional group to another on the basis of needs and accomplishment.

III. Meeting individual needs involves:
   A. the student's accepting an increasing responsibility for his education and becoming more active in the learning process.
   B. an educational program that is designed to fit the needs of the individual student.
   C. a learning process that occurs in a variety of ways, using many sources and resources.
   D. the staff's being regularly involved in assessing, prescribing, and evaluating the learning process.
   E. a broad and varied curriculum which offers choices and alternatives to the student.
   F. evaluative processes that reflect the objectives of the program with emphasis on the the individual needs and abilities of the student (policy provided by the district).

Amplifying on these goals and objectives, Doug Sebring, the district's coordinator for the gifted, emphasizes the school board's commitment to excellence and, at a more practical level, the flexibility of its scheduling. The school system provides funding to transport students where necessary and to continue classes at the secondary level with small enrollments. AP courses in calculus and physics, for example, may enroll only 6–8 students; pre-algebra in the middle school typically enrolls 2–8 students.

At the elementary level students functioning above grade placement may be served in cluster grouping within the class if the number of advanced students justifies such an arrangement. Or the students may move to another grade level for appropriate instruction. A magnet school for highly gifted students in grades one through five draws from all five elementary schools those students advanced at least 2 years beyond their normal grade placement. The magnet program, called the Advanced Study Program, compacts the usual curriculum content and accelerates students in order to provide additional enrichment opportunities. Students may progress as rapidly as their abilities allow because the same vertical acceleration is offered at the middle school.

Mathematically precocious elementary students may begin pre-algebra or algebra classes usually taught at the middle school. Most begin this advanced math in the fifth grade; some have successfully begun in the fourth grade.

At the middle school all entering sixth-graders are screened for inclusion in accelerated classes in math, science, foreign language, and language arts. Students who begin French, German, or Spanish in the sixth grade may complete 3 years of instruction in two languages or follow one language through 5 or 6 years. Those advanced in math can follow a sequence that will take them through 2 years of AP calculus. The more able science students are allowed to complete their middle school science in 2 years and enter a high school course in the eighth grade.

At the time of this report, the North Olmsted High School offered Advanced Placement courses in English, history, biology, chemistry, physics (A and B), calculus (AB and BC), and Spanish. AP courses in computer science and French were planned. In addition, the high school allows students to enroll concurrently at local colleges to obtain credit for transfer after graduation.

ROCKFORD PUBLIC SCHOOLS

The **Rockford** (Illinois) **Public Schools** District 205 combines an academic K–12 program for its intellectually advanced students with a creative and performing arts program for the artistically talented.

The combined programs serve approximately 4% of the district's 28,000 students. The program is centralized; students from all over the city attend six schools that house the program.

Selection for the academic program is based on testing: IQ, achievement testing, and school performance. Students must qualify or requalify for grades 1, 4, 7, and 9. In the creative and performing arts program students audition for admission. Normally students enter at grade 4, and placement decisions are made at grade 9.

Flexible pacing is a regular feature of these programs in the Rockford Public Schools; however, the materials used for acceleration are not the regular curriculum texts. In language arts/reading, for example, the district has a K–6 scope and sequence that accommodates individual differences yet provides continuity and flexibility. A diagnostic reading inventory is administered during the first 3 weeks of the school year. The end-of-book test for the child's grade level is administered to students who score above grade level on the diagnostic test. Students who score 85% or above on the end-of-book test are allowed to omit the grade-level basal reading materials. Their reading instruction consists of individualized reading programs and alternative basal reading materials that are above the child's grade placement.

In addition, a comprehensive K–6 literature program emphasizes reading and thinking at a variety of levels. Literary selections drawn from literary realism, fantasy literature, and traditional tales are analyzed for character, plot, setting, theme, style, point of view, and tone or mood. Appropriate higher-level thinking skills, such as critical reasoning, problem solving, and evaluation, are emphasized.

In mathematics flexible pacing is coordinated between Rockford and the Midwest Talent Search of Northwestern University (see Chapter 6 on Cooperative Programs). Students identified in the talent search may participate in a fast-paced Saturday morning math class, Algebra I–II–III. Those who do are exempt from their regular math class. A mentor is assigned to support each student. If this placement occurs during the eighth grade, the student's schedule in the ninth grade includes enrollment in a full year of honors geometry with the addition of Algebra IV in the spring semester. The student would then have one-semester courses in trigonometry and analytic geometry, followed by a full year of calculus. If a student takes the SAT during sixth grade and qualifies for fast-paced math during the seventh grade, the eighth-grade option is to attend high school for 1 or 2 hours per day to participate in the geometry/college algebra IV sequence. Such a student would complete mathematics through calculus in the sophomore year and then attend a local college for classes in mathematics.

Reporting for the Rockford Public Schools, Director of Gifted Programs Gary E. Heideman points out that in the last 5 years over 350 students have graduated from Rockford's gifted program. The classes of two recent years (1985 and 1986) have included students who began in the gifted program during elementary school. To document the long-range impact of the program, Heideman gives average scores over the last 5 years on the American College Testing Program (ACT) College Entrance Exams. The average composite scores on the ACT have risen steadily during this period, with a noticeable jump in the last 2 years:

Class of 1982	Class of 1983	Class of 1984	Class of 1985	Class of 1986
24.5	24.8	24.9	26.3	27.9

These composite scores put the Rockford students, on average, at the 95th national percentile. While it would be risky to claim a causal link between flexible pacing and rising ACT scores, school officials at Rockford are satisfied that their program is having a cumulative effect.

PLANO INDEPENDENT SCHOOL DISTRICT

Among the administrative complications introduced by a policy of flexible pacing is handling the transition between schools as students move ahead at individual rates, sometimes years ahead of their age-mates, often at different rates in different content areas. Policies and procedures adopted by the **Plano** (Texas) **Independent School District** serve both to illustrate the complications and to provide workable solutions.

In language arts the district has adopted a continuous progress approach in reading from kindergarten through eighth grade, and in spelling from kindergarten through sixth. By using team teaching the district can teach 10–12 levels of reading within a single grade. Typically one teacher on a team has had training in education of gifted students. The reading program can be accelerated; the basal readers through the eighth grade are reserved for the first six grades. Reading Coordinator Gerry Haggard reports that about one third of the sixth-grade students complete the eighth-grade basal reader. The district policy discourages radical acceleration, more than about one year ahead of grade level, but no student is ever prevented from moving ahead at a comfortable pace.

The reading activity is enriched as well as accelerated. Library reading and paperbacks are used to supplement the basal materials.

The Junior Great Books Program is incorporated in the reading program for able learners starting with the second grade.

Reading materials from science and social studies are included as well. The Junior Great Books Program is incorporated in the reading program for able learners starting with the second grade. Writing skills are emphasized throughout; the district uses computers for composing from kindergarten on. The Plano school district feels its continuous progress approach is on solid footing in the language arts. A similar approach to flexible pacing is just taking shape in mathematics and science.

To handle students beyond the elementary level, district policy is that, "The district will develop a plan consistent with Texas Education Agency regulations providing students, with parental permission, the opportunity to accelerate the programs of study leading to graduation" (policy adopted 6/11/85, provided by the district). Because students may move through the district curricula ahead of schedule, the district has developed extended instruction, "accelerated programs," to move middle school students into the high school curriculum when they are ready. For their 9th through 12th grade courses—except pre-algebra and algebra I, offered in the middle school—students who have completed the prerequisites may take advanced courses either at the middle school or at the high school, depending on where they are offered.

Because the middle school students who take advanced or accelerated courses are not in high school, the accelerated courses may not count toward the 21 or 22 units of credit required for graduation. Math courses above algebra I and foreign language courses above level I may be used to satisfy the mathematics or other-language requirements for graduation. If an advanced course is an honors course, it may count as one of the honors courses required for graduation under the Advanced High School Honors program.

Plano students sometimes participate in courses outside the school district's offerings. The district has had good experience with summer programs at Duke University and Southern Methodist University, offered to students identified in Duke's talent search among seventh graders. The district is confident that the objectives of these summer courses are equivalent to or beyond the objectives of corresponding high school courses. Students taking these courses may receive high school credit, satisfy graduation requirements, and earn grade points. Students taking courses in other university programs must take an examination to receive credit.

ARLINGTON INDEPENDENT SCHOOL DISTRICT

One of four school districts participating in the Pyramid Project (see Chapter 6, Cooperative Programs), the **Arlington** (Texas) **Independent School District** serves over 40,000 students, K–12. Having joined the Pyramid Project as part of its commitment to academic excellence, the district has targeted six elements to emphasize during its 5-year start-up phase: enrichment, flexible pacing, fast-paced compacted courses, accelerated content, advanced placement, and concurrent enrollment (except for enrichment, all these elements fit our definition of flexible pacing). Flexible pacing in reading and math is receiving particular attention in elementary schools throughout the district.

Principal Bob Windham, reporting for Ruth Ditto Elementary School, describes the flexible pacing approach in mathematics. Students are tested in May for inclusion in "Pyramid" groups for the following fall. To qualify, students must score 85% or higher on standardized tests and must have good work and study habits.

The pattern for these flexibly paced math groups is that they begin working in their grade-level texts, skipping many of the early review and facts chapters. As each group approaches a new chapter a pretest is administered. Those who score below 90% on the pretest cover the content of the chapter in a manner determined by the teacher. Those who pretest at 90% or above do project work, enrichment activities, and problem-solving tasks based on the content covered in the current chapter.

The method at Ruth Ditto Elementary, representative of the district's general approach, is not completely individualized. Although enrichment activities are tailored to the particular interests of the most proficient students, the class moves through the district's sequence of math skills together and at an accelerated pace. Some cross-grade-level assignments are made for unusually able students who would be held back even in an accelerated group working as much as a grade level above the normal classes.

To illustrate the special needs of students with exceptionally high abilities, Windam talks about Brian, a student who needed an individually tailored curriculum even before the flexible pacing program was introduced. In second grade Brian went to third grade for math instruction, where he was the best student in the top group. By the fifth grade Brian had completed the seventh grade math curriculum with the sixth grade "Pyramid" group. In the spring of

Brian's fifth-grade year, the principal, the parents, the district mathematics consultant, and the consultant for gifted students met with a representative from the junior high school. They decided that Brian should skip the sixth grade and go directly into seventh, and into eighth grade for mathematics.

Brian's double promotion necessitated some adjustments. He was at first mistakenly placed in an honors English class that proved too advanced for him. Some individual attention was needed in the math class to reinforce the math background Brian had covered at an accelerated rate. Once the adjustments were made, however, Brian flourished in the classes with older students. According to Windham, "The real key to this success was Brian's social and emotional development. His strong self-concept and maturity made this double promotion work."

As this story suggests, careful counseling and attention to individual needs are the key to successful alternate programming, including pacing adjustments. Arlington's statement regarding assessment considerations for flexible pacing in mathematics includes four elements:

1. *Reteaching.* If student performance indicates that the concept(s) may *not* be mastered, administer the Chapter-Review Test (Addison-Wesley) or Chapter Test (Harcourt) to identify weaknesses. These tests appear in the student edition of each text. Reteach using reteaching suggestions and worksheets provided. Then administer posttest.

2. *Mastery.* (a) If 90% or higher mastery is attained on the Pretest, record the score in the Posttest space. Move on *or* enrich. (b) If, after reteaching, a student does not attain 90% mastery level, the teacher should request a conference with the principal and/or vice principal and/or consultant to reevaluate the student's level and performance, checking for possible misplacement.

3. *Professional Judgment.* Liberally apply professional judgment when analyzing test results. Unsatisfactory performance on one test because of careless computational mistakes is not the same as habitual unsatisfactory performance because of lack of understanding of concepts or poor work habits.

4. *Clerical Assistance.* Consider assigning numbers to students for test-taking so that volunteers can assist in scoring of tests.

Important to the development of flexible pacing in Arlington are the staff development opportunities the district provides. The district's inservice training routinely includes attention to the goals of the Pyramid Project. The Arlington math teachers have been offered important assistance through the the staff development project described in Chapter 8 by Kathleen Martin. Language arts teachers receive Junior Great Books leadership training offered by the Gifted Students Institute. In addition, the Arlington district has assumed a serious commitment to the AP program. Junior high and high school teachers of English have attended a summer course in Teaching Honors and AP English, conducted on the campus of nearby Texas Christian University. The district regularly sponsors workshops on Advanced Placement conducted by the Southwest Regional office of the College Board. The success of the recent concentration on Advanced Placement at the secondary level is reflected in a dramatic rise in the number of Arlington students who take AP examinations. Over a 3-year period (1984–1987), the number of students taking AP tests doubled, from 169 to 338; the percentage of students scoring 3 or over increased from 72% to 78%; and the number of test scores of 5 jumped from 20 to 77.

LAS CRUCES PUBLIC SCHOOLS

When the **Las Cruces** (New Mexico) **Public Schools** designed its program for able learners in 1981, the planners decided on a structure that would combine enrichment opportunities in the regular classroom for students in all grades with the option of acceleration for those gifted students in need of faster-paced coursework. Accelerated pacing is a feature of the Advanced Education Program (AEP). Appropriate pacing is intended for all students, whether advanced or not.

Represented graphically, in Figure 2, the model for the education of students in the Las Cruces Public Schools resembles that of the Pyramid Project (see Figure 3) designed (later) by the Gifted Students Institute to implement the findings of the Richardson Study (Cox, Daniel, & Boston, 1985; see Chapter 6 on Cooperative Programs).

As we have suggested in our definition of flexible pacing, the practice can take a variety of forms: a student may be moved to a higher grade level to work with older students in one subject area or several, or advanced material may be brought down to a student who remains with age-mates. A student may be accelerated an entire grade level if that arrangement suits his or her abilities and needs, or a student may be allowed flexible entry into coursework not necessarily offered in the regular curriculum. Some students change schools to attend appropriate courses. Elementary students travel to junior high buildings, junior high students to high schools. High school students may travel between high schools for advanced coursework not available in their buildings, or they may enroll in college coursework for concurrent credit. Transportation, via taxicab or bus, is provided for students enrolled in courses on two campuses.

FIGURE 2

**Advanced Education Project
Las Cruces Public Schools**

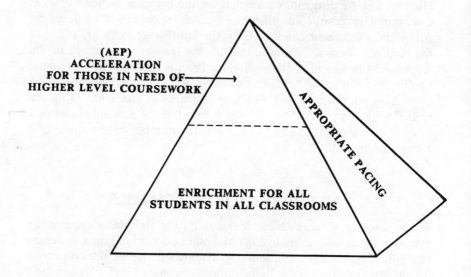

Former teachers have been hired by the Las Cruces Public Schools as AEP facilitators, to monitor student progress; to make arrangements for implementing student programs; to serve as a liaison between parents, teachers, and students; to hold individual and small-group meetings and address the affective needs of gifted students. The group meetings, called support groups, are essential to the program. They provide a forum for students to discuss and solve problems that arise among students participating in an educational program that differs from the norm.

The Las Cruces Public Schools have identified a number of elements they consider crucial to the success of a flexible pacing program that covers all grades of an entire district:

1. *A district advisory committee.* In Las Cruces the committee includes the associate superintendent of instruction, the directors of elementary and secondary curriculum, the coordinator of AEP, and their special student services director. This committee has the authority to make district-wide decisions such as allowing enrollment in more than one building, providing transportation between buildings, and giving credit for accelerated coursework.

FIGURE 3

The Pyramid Concept
Gifted Students Institute

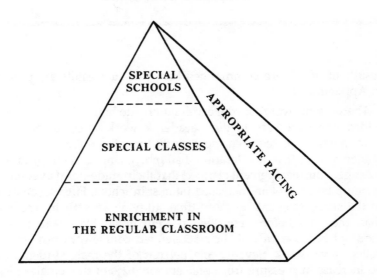

2. *Facilitators.* Each facilitator is assigned a caseload of about 35 accelerated students. The facilitators conduct the support groups, as mentioned above. Facilitators are not responsible for classroom instruction although they may occasionally serve as tutors.

3. *Credit.* Grades and credit are given on the student's transcript for the grade level at which a student would normally enroll in the class. For example, an 8th grader taking geometry at high school would be given high school credit for the course.

4. *Transportation.* As a public school obliged to provide appropriate education, the district must enable students to move between buildings.

5. *Support groups.* To meet the affective needs of students in the Advanced Education Program these groups meet weekly or biweekly at the elementary level, monthly at the secondary level.

In the spring of 1985 the Las Cruces schools had a population of 16,000 students. Of these, 550, roughly 3%, were in the Advanced Education Program. Seventy-one AEP students were in grades 10–12. A sample of 40 students was selected for an evaluation study, the

---

Students overwhelmingly enjoyed the widened friendship groups that came with acceleration into higher-level coursework.

---

results of which are summarized here (the full results are presented in Appendix C).

The students were asked if acceleration into higher-level coursework added more pressure to their academic work, affected their grade-point average, or required more study time. Fifty-nine percent of the students said that acceleration had not changed their grade-point average. Fourteen percent claimed that their grade-point averages had gone up because of an increased interest in school. Fifty-seven percent of the students spent no more time studying after their acceleration than they did before. Fourteen percent noted that more time was required because part of their accelerated coursework now included college-level work. Seventy-one percent of the male students noted no increase in pressure from acceleration; 62% of the females did feel an increase. An analysis of anecdotal responses indicated that females pressed themselves to make the top grades and felt some peer pressure as a result of being labeled "brain." The students were also asked to say which years in school and which academic courses had been so repetitive as to cause them to lose interest in school. Math, English, and science in grades 5–8 were seen by the students as the least satisfactory because they were the most repetitive.

The students were also asked to judge how acceleration had affected their social lives while in school. Most students in the group, 95%, felt they had an average-to-excellent social life. Sixty-seven percent felt their acceleration had not made their social life different from that of their non-accelerated peers. Of those who saw a difference in their social life, one student cited as a reason that he had ties in two schools; four felt their social life differed because they chose not to party with some of their peers. Only two students saw a difference in their social life because they were younger than their classmates. Ninety-two percent of the accelerated students viewed themselves as having several-to-many friends. Students overwhelmingly enjoyed the widened friendship groups that came with acceleration into higher-level coursework. Students who had been in the AEP only 1 or 2 years continued to identify with friends their own age; students who had been in the AEP 3 years or more identified more with their older friends. Almost all the the accelerated students, 95%, balanced their academic life with memberships in clubs, sports, or other activities outside of school. Approximately half of these students held positions of leadership in the clubs or other outside activities.

The responses of all the students surveyed indicated they felt more positive than negative effects from their acceleration. They appreciated the opportunity for early entry into more complex curricular structures and the elimination of repetition built into the regular curriculum. One hundred percent of the students in the study felt that if they had the choice to make again, they would still choose to accelerate.

The survey of Las Cruces students provides a useful and hopeful conclusion to our description of flexible pacing at all levels of a district. Personal responses do not constitute a scientific justification of flexible pacing. Such a justification awaits statistical data on a broad scale that will document the learning gains of accelerated students.

We have an intuitive sense that the more students master in the 13 years of their public schooling—the more proficient their skills, the more information they command, the more adept they are at integrating ideas from diverse domains—the more rewarding their education. This is largely a matter of definition; it has to do with what we choose to call a good education.

Our culture's lingering resistance to flexible pacing, including acceleration, is in part emotional. It is a combination of anti-intellectualism and misplaced egalitarianism, and it surfaces in a romantic attachment to intellectual innocence. As Joyce VanTassel-Baska has suggested, the schools themselves have "an age/grade obsession" tied to the convenience of selecting basal materials (VanTassel-Baska, 1986, p. 189).

It is refreshing and a confirmation of our belief in appropriate intellectual challenge that students who have been accelerated in their schooling do not feel persecuted or duped. In general they appreciate the challenge. They are pleased to acknowledge the honor. They would do it again.

CHAPTER 6

Cooperative Programs

The programs described in this section present a special case for flexible pacing. We start with the Center for Advancement of Academically Talented Youth (CTY), a university program that draws its students from a number of schools close to Johns Hopkins. Committed in principle to radical acceleration, CTY identifies students likely to profit from special attention and from the opportunity for unlimited accelerated advancement. The academic program, based squarely on the theoretical work of Julian Stanley, is weighted toward mathematics although it also includes special classes for the verbally gifted. We have chosen to highlight the Johns Hopkins program and the Model Mathematics Program (MMP), based on the Johns Hopkins program, to illustrate the results of a conspicuous and highly focused attention on mastery learning as a means of achieving continuous progress. The Johns Hopkins program and the MMP exemplify the confluence of theory and practice in a specialized field.

The other sections of this chapter touch on school-college connections and the broad, cooperative Pyramid Project. A theme running through this whole study is that our many educational institutions have the same goals. The size of the total enterprise, as well as its history, has resulted in a compartmentalization that probably impairs educational effectiveness. We can make education more coherent if we close the seams by working together.

THE JOHNS HOPKINS UNIVERSITY: CTY

The Center for Advancement of Academically Talented Youth has gained international recognition for identifying and working with

> *Committed in principle to radical acceleration,*
> *CTY identifies students likely to profit from*
> *special attention and from the opportunity for*
> *unlimited accelerated advancement.*

mathematically and verbally precocious youth. In 1971, The Johns Hopkins University pioneered the identification of mathematically talented adolescents with the founding of the Study of Mathematically Precocious Youth (SMPY) by Julian C. Stanley. Since 1979, CTY's national and international talent searches have identified more than 70,000 highly able students by inviting students 12 years old or in the seventh grade to take the Educational Testing Service Scholastic Aptitude Tests (SAT). Students so identified are offered a variety of academic opportunities, including the chance to attend CTY's summer residential and academic year commuter programs.

Classes for students younger than talent search age were begun in 1981 at Arizona State University under the direction of Sanford J. Cohn. Classes for students under 12 were offered for the first time at Johns Hopkins during the spring of 1985. Since then, a small number of summer and academic year commuter courses has been offered to students in the third through seventh grades. Young Students sites have been established in Baltimore, Maryland; Columbia, Maryland; and Richmond, Virginia.

Course offerings vary from site to site. They include a self-paced, individualized sequence covering arithmetic/pre-algebra/ algebra, reading the classics, basics of writing, Latin for language development, mathematical problem solving, and science exploration. In this section we confine our treatment to the mathematics program for 7- to 12-year-olds, second through seventh grades, conducted at The Johns Hopkins University campus in Baltimore. This program, begun in the spring of 1985, is representative, and it has useful links with school districts elsewhere in the region.

For selection of students CTY uses the School and College Ability Test (SCAT, developed by the Educational Testing service, published by Addison Wesley) to screen students identified by their parents or by their schools. Once in the program the students are tested for placement and for development of an individual educational plan, using the Sequential Tests of Educational Progress, Series II (STEP II, Addison Wesley). Small homogeneous clusters of students are assigned to separate teachers. Assignments range from one student to eight; most groups consist of three or four students.

---

*A student is not allowed to move ahead until he
or she demonstrates mastery either by
pretesting or by performance on homework
and testing.*

Classes are 2 1/2 hours, held on Saturdays for 24 weeks during the academic year. Students are instructed at levels appropriate to their achievement. They do in-class work and are assigned 3–4 hours of homework per week.

Testing is a critical part of this CTY program. Student progress and mastery of material is assessed weekly through homework, teacher-made and book tests, and standardized achievement tests. Records are kept of all homework, quizzes, and tests. Students are frequently pretested on new material, and instruction is geared to concepts and skills the student has not already mastered. A student is not allowed to move ahead until he or she demonstrates mastery either by pretesting or by performance on homework and testing.

Teachers in the program, usually undergraduate or graduate students, are chosen for their expertise in mathematics, their ability to communicate their knowledge to young children, and their acceptance of the CTY philosophy. Teachers go through an orientation and several training sessions, covering characteristics of the gifted, the CTY selection process, the math curriculum, testing procedures, and classroom methods. They meet with the coordinator of the program and a "master teacher" every week for evaluation of their teaching and their students' progress and for guidance.

Administrators of the program are highly trained and educated, with doctorates in psychology or education. They have a common goal and educational philosophy: to provide sound educational experiences at an appropriate level for intellectually talented students.

For evaluation of the program CTY examines the results of pretesting and posttesting to determine how many children have mastered their sequence of study and to assess each child's progress. All students are tested using out-of-level forms of the STEP test, minimally at the eighth-grade level. For most students this means that they are being tested two to five grade levels above their current grade placement in school. The students' test scores are then compared with the same above-level norms. Mastery is defined as 90th percentile with respect to these above-level norms.

For academic year 1985–1986 student progress ranged from 1 year to 3 years above grade level. Overall, only 5 students from an original enrollment of 59 failed to complete at least 1 1/2 years of math in 24 two-hour classes. One fourth grader mastered algebra I and algebra II and the next year went on to advanced algebra and geometry.

According to Sharon Higham, Director of Academic Programs for CTY, Brian is one of the brightest students in the Young Students Program. In his home school, a public elementary school, Brian is permitted to substitute his CTY math work for his regular school work. He may participate in his fifth-grade math class or go to a resource room and work on his CTY homework. Brian is well-adjusted socially and emotionally. He participates in extracurricular activities, including organized sports, and he has a wide circle of friends. Both his parents and his school take each day as it comes, allowing Brian to learn at his own pace without undue apprehension about "what will we do next year?"

Higham points out that some students experience difficulty in the CTY program. Some, for example, are inappropriately placed in the program. Occasionally, she says, a student's parents are the driving force behind the child's participation. Even with high ability, a student who would rather be playing soccer on Saturday mornings does not do well in the program. Higham says that occasionally CTY has admitted students who did not meet the cut-off scores for selection. Their parents or a teacher have insisted they belonged in the program. Almost always, she says, the test scores have been better indicators of potential success than these subjective judgments. The students' willingness is critical.

Another group of students who experience difficulty in the program or in later schooling are those whose home school will not accept or acknowledge their participation in CTY classes. These students must repeat work already covered, do double homework, and put up with harassment from teachers and (at times) administrators.

In general, with proper selection and placement and with a school system that is open minded and flexible, students show remarkable academic gains, renewed interest in learning, and heightened motivation to achieve. Moreover, their social and emotional development is enhanced. They meet and interact with other children who have similar abilities and interests. They feel accepted and "normal." By Higham's account, because their accomplishments are encouraged and highly regarded instead of resented and discouraged, CTY students develop an improved self-concept.

Student evaluations of the program are generally positive. They include such comments on the classes as "more challenging," "more fun," and "more interesting." Parents, says Higham, are overwhelmingly positive and thankful. The students typically have been bored and unchallenged in their school programs. Many of them are underachieving and are unenthusiastic about math. They may be perceived by their teachers as behavioral problems. Once in the CTY program the students discover renewed interest and excitement. If the home school accepts a child's CTY participation and accommodates its math instruction, the student's achievement and behavior improve markedly.

APPALACHIA INTERMEDIATE UNIT 8: MODEL MATHEMATICS PROJECT

That the Johns Hopkins approach can be transported and adapted to other settings is demonstrated by the success of the Model Mathematics Project under way in two rural school districts in Pennsylvania. The Hollidaysburg Area and Spring Cove School Districts set out to use the identification process and portions of the instructional design for mathematics developed at the Center for the Advancement of Academically Talented Youth.

Administrative arrangements were already in place prior to developing the Model Mathematics Project. Gifted students in the districts were served in a single location and grouped to facilitate individualized instruction. The teachers in the project were all experienced teachers of gifted youngsters, accustomed to using individualized, diagnostic-prescriptive instruction. The project offered staff development to acquaint the teachers with the Johns Hopkins model and the project's adaptation of it. Additional staff development was provided in evaluating student ability and achievement in mathematics, mathematics instruction for students highly able in mathematics, and prescribing mathematics instruction based on student assessments.

To find mathematically able students in a population of second through sixth graders identified as gifted, the project administered an in-level reasoning abilities test (SCAT). Those students scoring at or above the 95th percentile on in-level reasoning abilities were given an out-of-level test. Students who scored at the 50th to 74th percentile on out-of-level testing were grouped as highly able in mathematics (Group 3); those who scored at the 75th percentile and higher were identified as the most highly able in mathematics (Group 4). Students who did not meet the criteria for Group 4 or Group 3 were called Group 1 although there were actually two levels, 1 and 2. All students were given STEP tests to determine each student's present development in mathematics concepts and mathematics computation. An item analysis and mathematics profile based on the STEP were used to develop specific mathematics instruction for each student's individual education plan.

Instead of introducing a mathematical concept and then cyclically reviewing and further developing it, large blocks are constructed from the basal texts by combining topics from several levels into one instructional unit.

The Model Mathematics Project has created an instructional program differentiated for the varied ability levels in mathematics. The intent is not to erect a stratified system that limits students, but to provide instruction that will adequately challenge students. The program uses acceleration to establish the most appropriate instructional program for each student rather than expressly to accelerate them. The instructional program encourages students in Group 4 to advance according to their own ability and motivation in mathematics. It does not prohibit acceleration for students in Groups 1 and 3, but it recognizes that for able learners without unusually high ability in mathematical reasoning greater caution with acceleration must be maintained.

The mathematics textbooks already in place in each district are the backbone of the instructional portion of the project. Each classroom is supplied with a wide range of levels from the basal mathematics series so that each class can address a wide range of mathematical concepts. Students can work simultaneously from different levels in the math series. The scope and sequence charts that accompany each of the math series and daily logs of student progress are used to monitor each student's progress. Because the instructional program is individualized and many students progress through the basal content in a nonstandard fashion, accurate record keeping is essential. Test scoring, item analysis, and student profiles are maintained by a project coordinator.

A major feature of the instructional design of the Model Mathematics Project is that the mathematics curriculum is linearized for Group 3 and Group 4 students. The spiral approach built into the standard mathematics texts is straightened out. Instead of introducing a mathematical concept and then cyclically reviewing and further developing it, large blocks are constructed from the basal texts by combining topics from several levels into one instructional unit. Although students are continuously evaluated to assure retention, the linearization reduces the amount of review. The linearization is greater for students highly motivated in mathematics than for those less highly motivated and greater for students in Group 4 than for those in Group 3.

Each student's placement in the basal mathematics content and the specific mathematics skills to be developed are determined using the item-analysis profile from the STEP pretest along with pretests from the textbooks or assessments by the teacher. Each student's instructional program is individually prescribed according to the student's ability and motivation. Teacher-made and basal chapter tests are used as posttests to assess and document mastery of content. Ninety percent is regarded as the minimum level for mastery in the case of students progressing at an accelerated rate. The minimum mastery level for other students is set between 80% and 85%. Acceleration into an advanced grade level requires that the student's STEP scores be at or above the 90th percentile using fall norms for the higher grade level. If these conditions are met, no limit is placed on a student's advancement in mathematics.

The instructional design of the Model Mathematics Project has retained and expanded the enrichment component of the existing mathematics program. For students in Group 4 enrichment is less heavily emphasized and more accelerative in nature. In-level enrichment is a major component in instructional programs for students in Groups 1 and 3. Some areas of enrichment:

- Structure of mathematics
- Geometry
- Graphing
- Topology
- Problem solving
- Scientific and business applications
- Cultural aspects of mathematics
- Probability and statistics
- Patterns and relationships
- Computer
- Logic

Evaluation of the Model Mathematics Program has entailed both an analysis of pre- and post-achievement test data and a subjective survey of students, parents, and teachers. Although the project was not constructed with a formal research design, the test data lead to useful objective conclusions. For example, it has been possible to look for a correlation between high mathematical reasoning ability and IQ.

Although the average IQ increases as the mathematics ability of the group increases, the difference is small and not significant in the light of standard error of measurement of the tests used (see Table 2). This

TABLE 2

IQ for Mathematics Ability Groups

Group	IQ Range	Average IQ
4	131–166+	143
3	127–158	140
1&2	127–154	136

(IQ from Stanford-Binet or WISC, Revised)

information sheds light on the theory of multiple intelligences (Gardner, 1983) by suggesting that conspicuous achievement in mathematical reasoning is discrete from general intelligence.

As might be expected, those placed in the highest level to begin with show the most dramatic advances, but the quantity and quality of student content advancements has exceeded expectations in all groups (see Table 3).

Students made the largest achievement gains in mathematics computation. The average gain for students in Group 4 was approximately three times the expected or theoretical gain; that for students in Group 3, two times (see Table 4). Groups 3 and 4 also made significant achievement gains in mathematics basic concepts (see Table 5). For both Groups it was approximately 1.7 times the expected gain as predicted by national norms.

The subjective reaction of those involved in the Model Mathematics Project has been overwhelmingly positive. Surveys of the parents, students, and teachers indicate these results:

- There was better information about student ability and placement in mathematics.
- The Model Mathematics Project made the mathematics class more interesting and the overall experience was enjoyable.
- The students made greater progress in mathematics as a result of participating in the Model Mathematics Project.
- The students discussed mathematics activities more this year than they did formerly.
- Students' self-confidence improved because of participating in the Model Mathematics Project.
- Students were more interested in mathematics because of participation in the project.

- Students liked school more because of participation in the project.
- The Model Mathematics Project did not create frustrations in mathematics.
- Students did not have homework problems because of participation in the Model Mathematics Project.

Comments of teachers about their students give a sense of the benefits of the program. One teacher describes Sylvia as a talented second grader with excellent work habits and high level thinking skills. She is mature for her age. Sylvia works in a small group in her second-grade class with hands-on activities, computer problem-solving logic, and basic skills. She goes to third-grade math class two mornings a week, where she is given other challenging work and the opportunity to work with a more mature group. Sylvia's math interest has increased greatly. She enjoys school. She is moving through third grade materials and meeting the criteria set for her.

Fred is a sixth-grade student whose testing showed above-average ability in mathematics, but whose classroom performance was average. His attitude was passive and unconcerned. After only a week or so in the new program he started to push himself very quietly so as not to call attention to himself. After 2 1/2 months in the program he had completed almost a year's work. His testing placed him in an eighth grade pre-algebra program. Although Fred's ability is advanced, his performance is typical of students in the Model Mathematics Project. No longer merely the occupant of a seat in a math class, he became a participant in the math program. His resignation has been replaced by excitement and pride in what he is able to accomplish.

TABLE 3

Math Content Mastery for Students in Mathematical Ability Groups

Group	Average Advancement in Basal Mathematics Content (Three months instruction, mastery level = 90%)
4	1.3 years
3	1.0 years
1&2	0.4 years

TABLE 4

Student Achievement Gains in Mathematics Computation
Scores on STEP, Series II
(One Semester Instructional Period)

Group	Pretest Mean Conv.Score	Posttest Mean Conv.Score	Average Gain Conv. Score Units
4	439.0	450.2	+11.5
3	434.2	441.7	+7.5
1&2	434.2	438.3	+4.1
Theoretical Standard Group Grades 3–6	----	----	+3.8

TABLE 5

Student Achievement in Mathematics Basic Concepts
Scores on STEP, Series II
(One Semester Instructional Period)

Group	Pretest Mean Conv.Score	Posttest Mean Conv.Score	Average Gain Conv. Score Units
4	438.6	443.1	+4.5
3	432.0	436.6	+4.6
1&2	431.9	435.3	+3.4
Theoretical Standard Group Grades 3–6	----	----	+2.7

OTHER SCHOOL-COLLEGE COOPERATIVE EFFORTS

The work with academically precocious children at Johns Hopkins, including the talent search, has led to the establishment of similar searches and coordinated programs at three other university centers: Duke University, Northwestern University, and Arizona State University.

The Midwest Talent Search (MTS) at Northwestern University is representative. Joyce VanTassel-Baska's account of the MTS (1985) describes the benefits of the MTS and the other programs. She points out that the preferred program of these talent search centers is acceleration in traditional content fields rather than "enrichment" areas. She adds that universities cooperating with the talent searches are enabling qualified students to enter college level work, sometimes as early college entrants, sometimes under concurrent enrollment, and so shortening the time of their passage through the educational system.

Cooperation between schools and colleges to improve American education at all levels and in diverse elements of the process, from teacher training to improved administration to supplemental programming, is the subject of considerable attention in recent years. School-college liaisons were the subject of a study by the Carnegie Foundation for the Advancement of Teaching in the early 1980s (Maeroff, 1983). A conference at New Haven in November, 1986, sponsored by the Yale-New Haven Teachers Institute, featured some 19 programs of school-college cooperation around the nation (a personal communication included a list of projects, 1987; see also *Teaching in America*, 1983). An *Education Week* article on John Goodlad (Olson, 1987, published March 18, 1987) suggests that Goodlad is working to establish a network to foster such collaboration. Not all of these cooperative programs are tied essentially to accelerated learning or other forms of flexible pacing, but they are compatible with the concept and reinforce it by strengthening the links between high school and college pedagogy and content. Benbow and Stanley (1983) argue that entering college at a younger-than-average age can be advantageous for many able learners, whether moderately gifted or extremely precocious. Insofar as students accelerated by flexible pacing in any of its forms normally cross the boundary between school and college at an earlier age than most of their classmates, a spirit of cooperation, collaborative machinery, and understanding is crucial.

THE PYRAMID PROJECT

The Sid W. Richardson Foundation of Fort Worth, Texas, has taken the lead and set the pattern for another kind of inter-institutional cooperation that has far-reaching implications for public education. In 1981 the Richardson Foundation began a study of education for the nation's able learners that culminated in a report often referred to as the Richardson Study (Cox, Daniel, & Boston, 1985). An important early outgrowth of the Richardson Study was the Pyramid Project (Feldman, 1985).

Inaugurated in 1985 to implement the recommendations of the Richardson Study, the Pyramid Project is a cooperative effort among four school districts in the Dallas/Fort Worth metropolitan area: Cedar Hill (in a suburb south of Dallas), Birdville (in a suburban area adjacent to Fort Worth), Arlington, and Fort Worth. The districts range in size from Cedar Hill, with a student population of 2,300, to Fort Worth, with 65,000 students. The 5-year goal of the Pyramid Project is to launch comprehensive programs for able learners in the four districts. The long-range hopes are that the participating districts will maintain the comprehensive programs thus established and that the project as a whole will serve as a model for districts across the country.

Central to the Pyramid Project is its commitment to flexible pacing, a conviction that students should move ahead as they master content and skills. This commitment is built into the visual representation of the Pyramid Concept as the uninterrupted side panel of the pyramid (see Figure 2, p. 52). Each participating district initiated its 5-year plan with a determination to break the age-in-grade lockstep clearly in the foreground.

How the four school districts in the Pyramid Project have moved in the direction of flexible pacing need not be repeated. The continuous progress approach of Cedar Hill (High Pointe Elementary School) is presented in some detail in our chapter on Flexible Pacing at the Elementary Level. The Arlington district's success in working with nearby institutions is mentioned in our chapter on Flexible Pacing at All Levels. At the secondary level the four districts use options like those adopted by other schools across the nation, relying primarily on Advanced Placement courses and, in the case of Fort Worth, introducing the International Baccalaureate.

Some of the goals of the Pyramid Project have already been achieved. The study and the project have gained national attention. The Pyramid Project has extended its affiliations beyond the four original school districts. The Ardmore (Oklahoma) City Schools started a Pyramid Project of their own (see Chapter 3, Flexible Pacing at the Elementary Level), and the school district of Mineral Wells, west of Fort Worth, has a similar project under way. In addition, the model of cooperation between private foundation and public school district has been replicated in Florida, where the Bush Foundation has initiated a similar project in cooperation with the University of South Florida. The

Ardmore Pyramid Project was funded for its first 3 years by a grant from the Kerr and Noble foundations in Oklahoma.

For the purposes of this study the significance of the Pyramid Project is twofold. In the first place it illustrates what can be achieved by the infusion of private funding into public education. It is the vision of the Richardson Foundation's executive director, Valleau Wilkie, that a relatively small supplemental investment in a program already fully funded will yield significant results.

In the second place, the Pyramid Project illustrates the importance of cooperation among school districts and between school districts and other agencies. From its central position as coordinating agency, the Gifted Students Institute is able to broker staff development opportunities that can be shared by the participating districts. For example, the Gifted Students Institute, in cooperation with nearby Texas Christian University, has conducted summer institutes for teachers of honors and AP English that are available to all districts in the Dallas/Fort Worth area. Similar workshops concentrating on teaching methods as well as content have been offered to teachers of mathematics at the elementary and middle school grades and to teachers of foreign language (see Chapter 8 by Kathleen Martin). The institute conducts workshops training teachers in the use of Junior Great Books. And simply by coordinating the efforts of the participating districts, the institute becomes both locus and agency for cooperation among the districts.

In education, especially, cooperation is essential. We need all the help we can get.

CHAPTER 7

Selected Features of Flexible Pacing

In the preceding chapters we have looked at how flexible pacing is conceived and managed at various levels in different school settings. The schools and districts we have described offer practical solutions to typical problems, giving concrete demonstration that flexible pacing is educationally sound, is workable, and is being used in many locations in a variety of settings. In this chapter we pull the concept of flexible pacing apart to examine individual features. Here as before our focus is on the practical—what works, how it is done. But instead of looking at flexible pacing programs school by school, we look at flexible pacing element by element.

The features we have selected to concentrate on are suggested by the responses to our questionnaires. We have at our disposal not a comprehensive survey of schools across the country that practice flexible pacing in any of its forms but a sampling of schools, self-selected, that have told us how they conduct their flexible pacing.

The elements we consider in this chapter are (a) school or district policy, (b) student population served and degree of acceleration resulting from flexible pacing, (c) strategies of implementation, (d) methods of staff selection and staff development, (e) record keeping, (f) methods and results of evaluation, and (g) role of support mechanisms among parents, the community, and the school system.

SCHOOL OR DISTRICT POLICY

Despite a general concurrence among educational theorists that individuals learn at different rates and in different styles and the belief that the best educational programs are tailored to individual

---

*Flexible pacing will not occur systematically
or to any significant extent unless the school or
district has a policy that encourages,
preferably enforces, the practice.*

---

differences (Snow, 1986), it is safe to say that flexible pacing will not occur systematically or to any significant extent unless the school or district has a policy that encourages, preferably enforces, the practice. While the policies we have examined are not uniform, virtually all the successful schools and districts have tackled the matter at the policy level.

Sometimes the policy is dictated by the state education agency. California, for example, has a policy for its Gifted and Talented Education programs (GATE) that is of long standing. The San Diego Unified School District's Administrative Procedure Number 4236, adopted in 1962, revised in 1984, outlines nine programs specified by the state regulations. Although some of the enrichment programs and special classes do not result in flexible pacing, at least three allow students to move ahead as their achievement warrants: cluster grouping in regular classes, acceleration, and postsecondary education opportunities, including College Board AP classes.

According to GATE administrator David P. Hermanson, individual sites are responsible for the programs at the separate locations. The district offers guidance to help the schools develop written plans, including curriculum elements and staff development, that comply with state guidelines. The district cannot avoid giving attention to the most able learners, and flexible pacing is encouraged by the policy.

Jefferson County Public Schools, serving students in the area of Golden, Colorado, has a statement developed locally and adopted by its board of education in 1980. The district philosophy governing services to gifted students provides for a program composed of many options, administered in school-based variations. A more specific policy describing instructional strategies for continuous learner progress, adopted for implementation with the 1986–1987 school year, specifies that the instructional program will be "congruent with the developmental stages of the students being served"; that instructional arrangements will be organized and resources managed "in such a way that those resources are used most effectively to assist students in the learning process"; and that individualized instruction "will contain a continuum of learner objectives which will permit continuous learner progress and ensure continuity of learning for each student."

The Indian Hill Exempted Village School District, in Cincinnati, Ohio, has no specific mandate to offer flexible pacing. But the district's philosophy, policies, guidelines, long-range plans, and course of studies all contain the phrase, "to maximize student achievement." The district has interpreted this phrase to suggest flexible pacing. The policy governing the exceptional child, which covers children with physical or mental aptitudes significantly above or below the mean range for the district, allows placing students in district learning resource centers or outside the district in county facilities, vocational centers, or postsecondary educational institutions. Moreover, the policy governing the district's Discovery Class, for the talented and gifted, incorporates a sequential program in grades 1–7 with interdisciplinary themes to explore beyond the regular curriculum.

A similarly informal policy at North Central High School, in the Metropolitan School District of Washington Township, Indianapolis, Indiana, says that each student should be encouraged to advance at the student's own rate. According to James Hill, a department chair responding for the district, both school and district "have always operated under the philosophy that students should be placed according to their abilities. This has often resulted in very individualized programs of instruction for many students." In more concrete terms, North Central High School offers a wide range of accelerated courses, designated "X" courses, many of which culminate in AP credit by examination; North Central has initiated courses leading to the International Baccalaureate, beginning in the fall of 1987; and the school has a full program of individualized contract learning options to allow students to move beyond their grade level.

Kenwood Academy, an academic high school (grades 7–12) in the Chicago Public Schools, has been offering flexible pacing and an enriched curriculum since 1979. In 1986 the Chicago Board of Education adopted the recommendations of a city-wide task force on gifted education. Of particular interest are Recommendation 21, that "All proposals and programs for the gifted include both acceleration and enrichment (i.e., faster pacing and greater depth)," and Recommendation 34, which asks that 19 principles for the development, implementation, and evaluation of differentiated curriculum for gifted and specific aptitude/talented be adopted to serve as programmatic and operational guidelines. The guidelines include the principle of acceleration: "The pace of gifted programs for imparting knowledge and engendering basic skills should be radically accelerated over the pace common in programs for average children." The guidelines also honor the principle of significance, that "Gifted programs should deal with substantive issues," and the principle of depth, that "Gifted programs should involve gifted children in a quest for meaning, the extraction of abstract principles, and the entertainment of concepts of greater complexity than could be accommodated by average children of a similar age."

The striking feature of these policies governing education for able learners and resulting in flexible pacing is that most of them are of recent date. It is clear from our survey that across the country schools and districts are fairly recently becoming aware of the need to adjust pacing for superior students. It is a heartening sign.

POPULATION SERVED AND DEGREE OF ACCELERATION

The literature on education for highly able learners is spiced with tales of children of prodigious ability who have made dramatic academic strides, especially in mathematics. Jay Luo, who completed his baccalaureate degree at Boise State, Idaho, just after his 12th birthday, and Terry Tao, the precocious Australian youth whose mathematics ability attracted the attention of Julian Stanley, John Feldhusen, and other leaders in this field, are only two examples (Gross, 1986). For such students, specialized programs have been tailored to allow them to find intellectual challenge at whatever academic institution is appropriate, whether at a university or in their home school systems. Such students are rare, indeed.

Of more direct concern to educators at the school and district level are students whose needs and abilities are not so far out of the ordinary. We struggle to discover how to serve students whose abilities can and should be handled in the regular school setting even though they are misplaced in a classroom with youngsters their own age with more nearly average learning abilities.

This study began by looking at schools that use flexible pacing as a means of serving the needs of their abler students. Within the limited group of schools we surveyed, flexible pacing in its various forms is most often used in programs for identified gifted students. The Jefferson County Public Schools, for example, places about 2% of its student population in its program of Continuous Learner Progress for gifted and talented students. The New Durham Elementary School uses continuous progress only with its identified gifted and talented students. Their program has been in place for 6 years. In the year they report on, 18 of 160 students in the school (just over 11%) were offered flexible pacing. Of those, 14 (9%) were ahead by 1 year, the remaining four were advanced by 2 years (2.5% of the total).

Flexible pacing, including continuous progress, is not and should not be limited to the most able learners. The Las Cruces Public Schools strives to achieve appropriate pacing for all its able students. As they picture their program, using the pyramid figure (see Chapter 5 on

*Flexible pacing, including continuous progress,
is not and should not be limited to the
most able learners.*

Flexible Pacing at All Levels), enrichment activities are available to all students in the regular classrooms. The most able students, at the top of the pyramid, participate in the Advanced Education Program (AEP), which encourages acceleration and provides faster-paced coursework. According to the district's AEP facilitator Barbara Morrison, some 460 of the district's 17,300 students (roughly 2.7%) have this opportunity for accelerated learning.

For some districts flexible pacing is routine and has been in place for years. In Citrus County, Florida, the Lecanto Primary School has used continuous progress since the school opened in 1979. Mastery learning is encouraged at all grade levels (K–5) and across all content areas, but occurs most widely in the areas of reading and mathematics. According to Mary Bray and Colleen Passaro, reporting for the school, just over 11% of the students are advanced 1 year ahead of their grade level, and less than 1% are accelerated by 2 years.

While no reliable national figures can be given for the percentage of students who should be accelerated or by what amount they should be advanced, some noticeable patterns have emerged. The restricted data base on which our study is founded suggests that somewhere between 20 and 25% of the students in our public schools can handle material about a year ahead of where their age would place them. The number who can advance 2 or more years ahead of grade level is low, around 1 or 2%. Research is needed to determine what percent of students truly profit from accelerated pacing and what degree of acceleration will result from allowing students to advance at their own pace. The conclusion that seems to emerge from our survey is that the principal value of flexible pacing is not to be found in radical acceleration. It is instead to be found in appropriate challenge, what Halbert Robinson called "the optimal match" between a student's abilities and the pace of the schooling (Robinson & Robinson, 1982).

The phenomenon we discovered at Lowell Elementary in Salt Lake City, Utah, is instructive. There the EQUIP Program has been using continuous progress for 9 years, serving about one-quarter of its students. For just over 1 year the district has employed a continuous progress approach for all of its students, using teams of teachers and grouping students according to academic ability rather than age, in reading, language arts, and mathematics. Frequent assessment of students allows movement from group to group and so avoids the cumulative entrenchment effect of more rigid "tracking." The total school population profits from the lessons learned about flexible pacing in the EQUIP Program. Yet, the number of students advanced ahead of their grade level by 1 year is about 20%; the number of those accelerated by 2 years or more remains under 2%.

STRATEGIES OF IMPLEMENTATION

The anecdotal evidence of schools and districts we surveyed supports another observation about flexible pacing. Any change in the way students are advanced through the curriculum is likely to be introduced gradually and tried out with a selected population. The Ardmore, Oklahoma, City Schools set out to construct a system-wide program for its able learners by adopting continuous progress in mathematics in grades K–8 in all its schools. The task of articulating a sequential curriculum seemed more natural in math than in other subject areas. They developed a record-keeping system and a means of tracking the progress of individual students along the math continuum that helped them extend flexible pacing into the language arts the following year. At the time of writing, flexible pacing was under way in language arts, with a similar approach for social studies projected for the following year. In none of these academic areas is flexible pacing limited to the academically superior students.

A slightly different, but equally deliberate, approach has enabled the Cedar Hill Independent School District, near Dallas, to implement flexible pacing one step at a time. As the Cedar Hill district expands by adding new elementary schools, it adopts continuous progress in each new school. The district will extend continuous progress into the established schools only when the newer schools have a record of success and enough experience with the logistics of flexible advancement to make the transition easy for the older schools.

Other procedures that might be considered under the rubric of implementation strategies are implicit in several sections of this chapter. We have already mentioned that flexible pacing will most likely be realized only if the district school board or the school administration adopts a policy requiring appropriate pacing and the leveling of instruction according to each student's ability and achievement rather than age. In the sections that follow we discuss record keeping and evaluation, both crucial to the task of persuasion that enables flexible pacing to take place. In our final section we discuss support mechanisms that contribute to the success and also the general acceptance of a program of flexible pacing.

METHODS OF STAFF SELECTION
AND STAFF DEVELOPMENT

To allow students to move through the school curriculum at their own pace requires a complex commitment from every teacher. First, each teacher must agree that the best way to serve students is to allow them to progress in key subject areas as they master content and skills. The teachers must recognize that as a consequence students will be placed for instruction with other students at the same curriculum level, not necessarily those of the same age. As the history of American education makes clear, not all teachers accept this starting position.

If the school or district has a policy that flexible pacing will govern the placement of all or a portion of the students, it is likely that teachers will accept the provision. But accepting that students should be allowed to move at their own pace is only the beginning. Given the backgrounds and training of most teachers, a shift to flexible pacing normally requires retraining in the teaching methods and classroom management that allow some form of continuous progress.

Among the schools and districts we surveyed, the training of teachers usually assumes a pattern of sending teachers to conferences on selected topics, such as education of the gifted; inviting outside consultants to introduce methods of grouping, team teaching, and curriculum sequencing; and conducting inservice training on a variety of topics specific to pacing. The Lowell Elementary School in Salt Lake City, for example, has its staff attend a week-long conference on gifted education held annually at Utah State University. At New Durham Elementary School, in New Durham, New Hampshire, teachers attend district-wide inservice days for all teachers (K–12), covering a variety of topics, including flexible pacing and differentiating curriculum for able learners.

Conspicuous among these efforts at staff development are a number of cooperative programs involving the schools and districts with nearby colleges and universities. The Cedar Hill Independent School District, near Dallas, Texas, provides funds for teachers to enroll in university courses addressing the improvement of instruction for high-ability students. The Ardmore City Schools in Oklahoma have worked closely with an area college to offer college-credit courses through the higher education center in Ardmore. The Claremore School District, also in Oklahoma, held a two-credit graduate seminar, in the summer, on the Walter Leeper Middle School campus, conducted by a professor from Northeastern Oklahoma State University. The Las Cruces public schools has augmented its inservice in gifted education, conducted by Joyce Juntune, Carol Schlicter, and other educators of national stature, with 15 hours of university-level independent study in the area of gifted education.

---

*The most prevalent pattern of staff development
is what might be called "in-house" activities.*

At the secondary level, summer institutes that prepare teachers for the College Board's Advanced Placement courses or the International Baccalaureate are well established and are centered on single disciplines. These cooperative programs contribute by helping teachers address the needs of advanced high school students undertaking college-level coursework on their high school campuses.

The most prevalent pattern of staff development is what might be called "in-house" activities. Lecanto Primary School, in Citrus County, Florida, has sessions developed by its own faculty on such topics as team teaching, meeting the needs of slow learners, learning centers, individualizing instruction, and teaching children to think. Mast Way Elementary School, in Durham, New Hampshire, has similar development activities developed locally. Walter Leeper Middle School supplements its summer seminar with inservice sessions conducted by its program steering committee and the school principal during regular and special faculty meetings.

No one of these approaches to staff development is uniquely appropriate. Typically a school district will combine them in ways determined by the circumstances and the personnel. In the North Olmsted City Schools, in Ohio, teachers and administrators are encouraged to attend and to present at state and national conferences. Such professional interaction stimulates creativity and enables the teachers and administrators to see their own programs critically. Cooperative programs sponsored by local universities and educational foundations have enabled many staff members, particularly those in the program for the gifted, to acquire current information on what is being done elsewhere. Each building has its own staff development plan to serve its special needs. In the Rockford Public Schools District 205, in Rockford, Illinois, staff development activities draw on regular grade-level meetings and workshops, outside consultants, and an artist-in-residence. Teachers in the gifted program, where the flexible pacing option is in place, meet Illinois teacher reimbursement qualifications, which include a graduate course in gifted education, a Level I–II workshop in programmatic options for gifted students, or 2 years of experience in working with identified gifted students.

The CTY program conducted by The Johns Hopkins University is a special situation. The administrators of the program are specialists with doctorates in psychology or education. All subscribe to the goal of the program: to provide sound educational experiences at an appropriate level and pacing for intellectually talented students. Teachers in the program, chosen for their expertise in mathematics, their ability to communicate their knowledge to young children, and their acceptance of the CTY philosophy, go through an orientation session and several training sessions. They meet weekly with the coordinator of the program and a "master teacher" for guidance and for an evaluation of their teaching and of their students' progress.

In the Model Mathematics Project, based on the CTY model and conducted by Appalachia Intermediate Unit 8 of Hollidaysburg and Spring Cove, Pennsylvania, teachers were selected for their experience in teaching the gifted and their ability to deliver individualized, diagnostic-prescriptive instruction. The project offered staff development covering the Johns Hopkins model, the Model Mathematics Project, evaluating student ability and achievement in mathematics, mathematics instruction for students highly able in mathematics, and prescribing mathematics instruction based on student assessments. Most of these topics were repeated in staff development meetings with guidance counselors, principals, and other administrators from the two school districts.

RECORD KEEPING

Record keeping is a major concern for any school or district that allows flexibility in instructional arrangements. To illustrate briefly we summarize here the 9-point assessment and record-keeping guidelines used by the Arlington (Texas) Independent School District for its flexible advancement math, grades 1–3. Each teacher must:

1. Administer the end-of-year test to designated students.
2. Score tests and record the pretest scores on individual record cards.
3. Follow the sequence of the book at the appropriate level.
4. Administer free-response chapter test before the beginning of each chapter.
5. Score tests and record pretest scores on individual record cards.
6. Teach through direct *instruction*, provide *practice* and *enrichment*, then *test*.
7. Administer multiple-choice chapter test at the end of each chapter.
8. Score tests and record posttest scores on individual record cards.
9. Move on.

At the end of each unit those students who have achieved 90% mastery are allowed to move on; those who do not are retaught.

As this list of steps suggests, keeping track can be a headache, and the more flexible the system, the more detailed the record-keeping needs. One might suppose that the larger the unit of management, the greater the headache. And yet the attitudes of the responding schools vary widely. At one extreme we find the simple mechanics of the Lowell Elementary School in Salt Lake City: "Individual folders are kept on each student which track their progress in each subject area based upon the level of difficulty of materials used. These folders follow students from team to team." At the other extreme we find a level of automation that makes High Pointe Elementary School a major consumer of software. And the Leeper Middle School of Claremore, Oklahoma, takes some pride in its computerized record keeping: "A small grant obtained by Dr. Larry Howard allowed Mr. Kenneth Ralph, husband of a committee member, to design a program to facilitate sorting and placement of students by skills to appropriate teachers." The statement goes on to say that Mr. Ralph is planning to automate the grouping tasks.

Nothing in the responses we received suggests that the kind of information entered into the computer is different from the kind of information kept in individual folders. Two generalizations emerge from our look at this aspect of flexible pacing. One is that whatever record-keeping methods are used, the assessment of student progress still relies on the professional judgment of the teacher. The other is that as the technology of record keeping becomes more familiar, we are likely to see increased reliance on the computer and with it increased refinement of detail.

METHODS AND RESULTS OF EVALUATION

In the questionnaire we sent to schools participating in our survey we asked about procedures used to evaluate the program of flexible pacing. Our intention was to dissociate program evaluation from success stories or figures illustrating the progress of individual students. Anecdotes about the startling advances of the odd genius or accounts of the special chemistry of an isolated class, we felt, would not illuminate the broader issues associated with flexible pacing as an educational strategy.

But we also asked for case studies, and the responses we received mixed evaluations of program effectiveness with reports on the progress of the students. It may be that the most telling measure of a

If the method is successful, the magic of the individual classroom will result in an observable increase in the pace of learning for all students.

program's success is in the individual success stories. It is precisely the achievement of the uniquely precocious student that makes the case for flexible pacing. If the method is successful, the magic of the individual classroom will result in an observable increase in the pace of learning for all students. Some, but not all, will leap ahead dramatically.

The best documented and most widely known of the programs that use flexible pacing is at the Center for the Advancement of Academically Talented Youth (CTY) at The Johns Hopkins University. The procedures for evaluation at CTY will serve as a model against which to measure other programs. Started in 1985, the program at Johns Hopkins is still fairly new, but it has grown out of the Study of Mathematically Precocious Youth (SMPY), which has a track record of some 16 years and which has provided much of the statistical foundation for flexible pacing, particularly for acceleration of students with unusually high reasoning abilities in mathematics.

The evaluation procedures used at CTY have three distinct elements. The first and most objective is the testing of student achievement (see Chapter 6 on Cooperative Programs). For the year on which CTY reported, 1985–1986, student progress ranged from 1 year above grade level to about 6 years above grade level. One of the youngest students, then a second grader, completed the arithmetic/pre-algebra sequence in 1 year and went on to study algebra I in the next year. A fourth grader mastered algebra I and algebra II in 1 academic year and went on to study advanced algebra and geometry. Overall, 54 out of 59 students completed at least 1 1/2 years of math in 24 two-hour classes:

- Eleven students completed 1 1/2 years of math.
- Seventeen students completed 2 years.
- Fifteen students completed 3 years.
- Eleven students completed over 3 years of math.

The remaining five students dropped out of the program for various reasons.

The second element in the CTY evaluation process is administration of student and parent questionnaires. Students are asked to subjectively evaluate their math class and their teacher. Parents are asked to complete a questionnaire designed to assess course content, instructor, and course experience. Open-ended comments are encouraged. Both student and parent responses are highly positive.

In addition to the objective and subjective measures of success, the CTY has a follow-up survey it has mailed to former students. The program is too new to have results from this longer-range assessment. As data accumulate, the staff of CTY will be interested in benefits to the students that can be attributed to their participation in the CTY Saturday program. They will look with particular interest at advanced placement and content acceleration and will monitor other social, academic, and intellectual gains as well.

The nearest copy of the CTY model in a conventional school setting is the Model Mathematics Project (MMP) at Appalachia Intermediate Unit 8, in Pennsylvania. After 1 year the project was evaluated through an analysis of pretest and posttest data. The results of the pretest/posttest evaluations, presented in our chapter on cooperative programs, can be summarized briefly here: students in the two highest ability groups advanced in their mathematics computation by two to three times the expected gain; they advanced in mathematics basic concepts by 1.7 times the expected gain. The gains in these areas made by students in the lower ability groups were about the same as those of a theoretical standard group.

At the end of the year the students, parents, and teachers responded to a survey with more subjective evaluations, providing necessary support for the continuation of the program. Among the recommendations of the project supervisors, based on the responses to the survey, were the following:

- An existing mathematics program philosophically and pedagogically similar to that required by the MMP.
- Necessary staff expertise in gifted education and in the use of diagnostic-prescriptive instructional design.
- An IEP process to structure an individualized program for each student involving the parents.
- The support of the school district and a commitment to continue the program, in spirit and in fact, into the junior and senior high schools.

Evaluation results from schools and districts with more nearly comprehensive programs of flexible pacing follow a similar pattern. At Lecanto Primary School in Citrus County, Florida, for example, analysis of the results of the Comprehensive Test of Basic Skills reveals that students at Lecanto Primary performed better in reading, writing, and mathematics than the norms would predict. (See Table 6.)

A useful subjective evaluation was undertaken by the Las Cruces Schools, which surveyed high school students concerning their

TABLE 6

Results of Comprehensive Test of Basic Skills at Lecanto Primary

Grade	Area	1986 Grade Equivalent
1	reading	2.1
	language	2.3
	math	2.5
2	reading	3.3
	language	3.5
	math	3.3
3	reading	4.2
	language	4.2
	math	4.4
4	reading	5.6
	language	6.3
	math	5.5
5	reading	6.8
	language	7.2
	math	6.7

perception of the academic and social effects of acceleration. The results of that survey are included in Chapter 5 on Flexible Pacing at All Levels. The most significant finding of the Las Cruces survey was that students are uniformly positive about their experience with acceleration. One hundred percent of the students surveyed felt that if they had the choice to make again, they would still choose to accelerate.

To make a compelling case for flexible pacing or to demonstrate its impact, the most important information must be gathered over the long term. Years of improved achievement must be the goal of flexible pacing, not the occasional success story. Such achievement inevitably takes years to document. Long-range evaluation requires planning and is best built into a new program from its inception. An instructive model is provided by the Ardmore City Schools, where an evaluation plan, projected from the beginning, includes collecting data on student

One hundred percent of the students surveyed felt that if they had the choice to make again, they would still choose to accelerate.

achievement, gathering subjective responses from students and parents and the community as well, and building a record of the program's ability to attract attention outside the immediate community. Nine broad evaluation questions cover such concerns as where students score on standardized achievement tests at each stage of the project and to what degree the more able students are mastering high-level thinking skills. Subjective responses are to be gathered with surveys staged over the duration of the project. The important element of community attitudes and the experimental project's ability to garner favorable publicity reflects the district's awareness of the pragmatic need for community support.

ROLE OF SUPPORT MECHANISMS

In our description of flexible pacing at the Las Cruces Public Schools we mentioned the facilitators, former teachers hired by the district, who contribute significantly to the success of the Las Cruces program. Among their responsibilities is to hold small group meetings, called support groups, to deal with affective needs of the students and provide a forum for discussion of problems perceived by the students. This mechanism at Las Cruces represents the institutional side of the support needed to make an innovative educational approach work effectively.

The policies of the Indian Hill Exempted Village School District, Cincinnati, Ohio, indicate the range and kind of support services students need to cope effectively with their schooling, particularly if their education program takes them out of the expected pattern. The policies of Indian Hill require a placement committee to deal with special needs of any exceptional child, whether the child's abilities are significantly above or below the normal range. The guidance services provided by Indian Hill provide both academic or career counseling and individual or small-group counseling services that enable students to discuss their concerns openly and to explore with help their personal and social problems.

Not the least of the challenges associated with flexible pacing and multiple educational options are providing transportation to other sites for appropriate courses and allowing classes to be held with small enrollments. Transporting students from site to site is a logistical problem mentioned in the responses of both the North Olmsted City Schools (Ohio) and the Las Cruces Public Schools (New Mexico).

How a district or school handles counseling and other emotional support depends in large measure on the scale of the institutional machinery. At the New Durham Elementary School in New Hampshire the approach is informal. In a small school of 160 youngsters every staff member, including aides and support staff, works directly with the children. All are available as mentors and instructors; all see the youngsters every day and are involved in their projects.

An additional resource available to all schools and used effectively by many is the parents of the school children. A useful illustration of how parents can be conscripted and involved in the education of their youngsters is presented in a handbook for parents of students in the EQUIP Program of the Salt Lake City School district. This optional program for academically accelerated students is represented earlier in our study by the Lowell Elementary School of Salt Lake City. The Salt Lake City Board of Education expects parent participation in the classroom of any optional educational program.

Parents of EQUIP students are urged to provide 3 hours of cooperative assistance per week for the first child, plus 2 additional hours for the second child and 1 hour for each additional child in the program. The "co-oping" hours, arranged between the parents and the children's teachers, are given primarily to class participation. Parents may teach a subject, teach a short-term unit or mini-class, serve as classroom aides, or help with the preparation of programs or presentations. Parents unable to be on site make special arrangements to fulfill their obligation with committee work, telephoning, or other help that can be performed at home. The Salt Lake City school board feels that parent involvement is the most significant benefit of the EQUIP Program. It substantially improves the interaction of students and teachers, at the same time allowing the parents to evaluate and participate in their children's education.

Other illustrations of effective community support have been presented earlier. The conception and design of a computerized record-keeping system for the Walter Leeper Middle School by the husband of a staff member in the school is a small but important example of such cooperation. No one can pay for such concern, yet every school depends on some kind of volunteer effort. On a larger scale, the involvement of the private Richardson Foundation in public education is a signal example of what can be achieved when the boundary is breached between public and private institutions (see Chapter 6 on Cooperative Programs).

We have put the support element last among the features of a flexible pacing program, just before concluding and summing up, because it is crucial to the success of any educational project. The need for sound support from parents and the community is not peculiar to flexible pacing or to programming for able learners. It is central to all educational programs. A historical perspective helps to explain just why external support is so crucial to the classroom teacher. It was the growth of our population and the clustering of our people in urban centers that originally replaced the one-room schoolhouse of a century ago with the large, compartmentalized institutions that now conduct education on a massive scale. The sheer scale of public education in the 20th century is beyond our ability to control. The attendant bureaucracy and logistics present nearly impossible barriers to effective instruction.

Nothing has altered the intimate relationship of teachers and students in individual classrooms. But the multiplicity of classrooms and the range of ability levels have created a need for standards and put a premium on coordination and cooperation. Simple quantity has increased the complexity of the enterprise. In this context the cooperation of parents and the community, and their understanding of the demands on a teacher's time, can go a long way toward overcoming the impediments. The education of our young citizens depends importantly on matching the pace of instruction to the learning abilities of individual students. The goal is important and it depends on the whole society.

CHAPTER 8

Toward Improved Instruction for Mathematically Able Students

Kathleen Martin

To fit the practical bias of this study—to make it more concrete and move it one step in the direction of a how-to manual—we have asked Kathleen Martin to describe a staff development program that will prepare teachers to offer flexible pacing—in this case a continuous progress approach to mathematics instruction.

Like the rest of this study, Kathleen Martin's approach is based on what works, what is being done. Herself a college professor engaged in research on instruction in mathematics, Martin has conducted training for teachers in the Pyramid Project districts. In this connection, she has assisted the Fort Worth Independent School District in developing longitudinal staff development that resembles that of her hypothetical model.

The program Dr. Martin describes shares the premises that undergird the rest of this study. It assumes that curriculum design and teaching methods are the responsibility of the teachers and that teachers must bring to their task the best that is currently known about how students learn. It makes a strong case for cooperation among all constituents of the educational system, with parents and administrators supplementing and supporting the classroom interaction of teachers and students.

The fundamental condition on which this mathematics program depends is teamwork among those involved in mathematics instruction. If continuous progress is to fit its name, we must eliminate the boundaries between stages in the mathematics curriculum. To do so requires that all teachers understand the full range of mathematics development from the beginning to whatever point students can reach before going on to college. Moreover, to ensure that learning is sustained and reinforced, every student, especially those most able, must have support and encouragement at home as well as at school. Parental involvement is vital.

Martin's program entails a reexamination of the machinery of instruction. We must evaluate our textbooks and other instructional materials. We must reassess assessment. Both the instructional materials and our methods of assessment must serve the curriculum rather than determine it. Only if we base our mathematics instruction on a solid understanding of how students learn can we develop a mathematics program that allows student to learn all that they are able.

Neil Daniel
June Cox

In a recent report on the K–12 mathematics curriculum, a task force of the Mathematical Sciences Education Board includes the following recommendations:

New curricula cannot be implemented in a vacuum; one aspect of this is the necessity for reforming textbooks, tests and teacher education at the same time as we develop a new curriculum; another aspect is to involve all constituencies who will determine the success or failure of a new curriculum at an early stage and to keep them all involved throughout the process (Mathematical Sciences Education Board, 1987, p. 19).

These comments suggest that even the best planned curriculum of competent professionals faces serious challenges in implementation. Curriculum development, in itself a mammoth undertaking, is only a prelude to educational reform. Transforming classroom environments in ways that enable children to benefit most from a new curriculum requires significant changes in school policy and in instructional practices.

Julian Stanley has identified the age-in-grade lockstep as one of the school's organizational elements most in need of restructuring (Stanley, 1980, p. 11). Stanley suggests longitudinal teaching teams that would span kindergarten through the 12th grade and ensure the continuous mathematical progress of the students in their charge. While Stanley's recommendation is for the mathematical education of gifted students, it offers an appropriate model for education in every subject area. Flexible pacing through an educational continuum can begin to assure that students will receive suitable instruction at every level of their development.

In an earlier publication (Cox, Daniel, & Boston, 1985), the authors invented an imaginary school district through which they attempted to illustrate a comprehensive program for educating able learners. Some of the provisions included in that imagined program were drawn from descriptions of programs they found in real school districts. I use a similar approach in this chapter. I intersperse the hypothetical model with illustrations from a real project in the Pyramid districts (see Chapter 6 on Cooperative Programs) and related activities of the Fort Worth Independent School District (FWISD), a school district whose description parallels that of the hypothetical district. The math component of the Pyramid Project is one of 23 national exemplary projects funded under Title II's Educational Economic Security Act. It has recently achieved recognition as one of nine programs to be examined in a "Study of Disadvantaged School Districts Serving High Ability Students in the Fields of Mathematics, Science, and Foreign Language" under the sponsorship of the U.S. Department of Education.

Imagine a hypothetical school district located in a city of about 400,000, with a student population of almost 60,000. Some 60 elementary schools, 20 middle schools, and 10 high schools reflect a mix of ethnic cultures and socioeconomic strata. Within this network of schools, focus on a single feeder system consisting of one high school, the two middle schools whose students feed that high school, and six elementary schools whose students funnel into the middle schools. In this pyramid-like assembly of schools will be constructed a K–12 mathematics program to provide for the continuous progress of all students in those schools. Pay particular attention to the ways our program serves those learners who demonstrate exceptional ability in mathematics.

Following the recommendation of the task force of the Mathematical Sciences Education Board, we will structure our initial planning team to include all constituencies who will determine the success of a new curriculum. At the district level, members will be the Associate Superintendent of Curriculum and Instruction and the Director of Mathematics. Building level members will include the principals and one mathematics teacher each from the high school, middle schools, and elementary schools participating in the project. A math educator from a local university will complete the planning team.

Provisions for staff development are the most critical dimension of planning. Significant changes in curriculum and instruction cannot occur unless teachers are prepared to produce them. In its publication *Providing Opportunities for the Mathematically Gifted*, the National Council of Teachers of Mathematics (NCTM) states that "a solid program requires long-term planning beyond the scope of one teacher in a single classroom or even of a group of teachers at a single grade level" (House, 1987, p. 31). A lack of continuity and inadequate preparation of mathematics teachers are identified as two of the most pressing issues facing those interested in providing a quality mathematics program for able learners.

In elementary schools teachers tend to be less confident in teaching mathematics than other school subjects:

> Often they have minimal background in mathematics and may even dislike and fear the subject. Such teachers are only comfortable teaching mathematics in a very prescribed, algorithmic fashion, and they are unlikely to welcome the types of activities which require background in mathematics, a spirit of inquiry, enthusiasm for the subject, and problem-solving skills. They may prefer the safer route to providing for the gifted by using a higher grade textbook to teach more advanced computation (House, 1987, p. 58).

The NCTM statement has been validated repeatedly by more than 150 elementary teachers who have participated in the Pyramid Project's

*The re-education of elementary school
teachers is essential to any significant reform of
the mathematics curriculum.*

mathematics component. As part of the staff development, the teachers keep a journal in which they record and reflect on classroom implementation of concepts and corresponding activities learned in class. Almost without exception the journals reflect discomfort in teaching mathematics resulting from a lack of confidence. These same teachers point to an increase in security as the most significant change attendant upon mastery of mathematical concepts.

Whether the lack of confidence among elementary teachers teaching mathematics is a function of inadequate teacher education programs or whether elementary school teaching attracts less math-oriented people is not clear. It is clear, however, that the re-education of elementary school teachers is essential to any significant reform of the mathematics curriculum. For educating mathematically gifted youngsters, the problem is magnified. The NCTM publication points out that "the special abilities of the gifted and talented require programs that provide opportunities to develop abstract thinking, to sharpen higher cognitive processing, to practice creative problem posing and solving, and to enlarge individual methods and styles of inquiry" (House, 1987, p. 31). Teachers who respond to these special needs must know even more mathematics than their counterparts.

While teachers in middle school and high school might be expected to possess greater confidence, the evidence of national assessments indicates that such is not the case. The Second International Mathematics Study describes how mathematics is taught in the eighth grade in the United States:

> The most common overall pattern of teaching seemed to be a focus on the textbook and on the abstract and symbolic with an emphasis on rules and definitions imparted through a "show and tell" style (Crosswhite, Dossey, Swafford, McKnight, & Cooney, 1985, p. ix).

The description is telling in the contradiction between "abstract and symbolic," pointing to high level thinking, and "rules and definitions," imparted in a copy-cat style that requires the least intellectual effort. Such teaching leaves the mathematically promising students without stimulation or challenge.

Staff development is undoubtedly the most important item on our planning team's agenda. The size of our hypothetical district, however, combined with the likely rate of teacher turnover, argues against retraining all teachers at once. Our planning team, therefore, will choose an approach to staff development which will have a ripple effect. A cadre of 18 mathematics teachers—2 from our one high school, 4 from our two middle schools, and 12 from our six elementary schools—will constitute the training core. These 18 teachers will be provided systematic, in-depth training in K–12 mathematics education. Our teacher force will then be expected to become instructional leaders at their respective schools.

The staff development model actually in use in Fort Worth resembles that of our hypothetical district. Two high school mathematics teachers and two middle school mathematics teachers are working with a university mathematics educator. Together they are preparing 20 elementary school teachers to become instructional leaders in their own schools and to assist in the training of other elementary teachers throughout the district. These 20 elementary teachers are among the 150 who participated in a graduate course in the teaching of elementary school mathematics. All demonstrated enthusiasm for teaching mathematics and a particular aptitude for working with mathematically able children and with their professional peers.

One limitation of the Fort Worth mathematics project is that the teachers are drawn from elementary schools throughout the district rather than from a single feeder system as in the hypothetical model. While breadth may be achieved, depth is lost. Articulation between grade levels, especially between elementary school and middle school and between middle and high, is difficult to achieve in such a spread of personnel. Our hypothetical staff development model more closely approximates one of Stanley's longitudinal teaching teams. The team's overall responsibility is to guarantee the continuous mathematical progress of all students by communicating between the grade levels.

Since staff development is crucial to the success of our hypothetical model, a full academic year will be committed to the process. The planning team must ensure that participating teachers receive necessary support during this preparation period. Support includes released time from teaching assignments, preferably scheduled toward the end of the school day so that all teachers can be assembled regularly for joint instruction and ongoing curriculum development.

In the FWISD mathematics project, staff development is an add-on for teachers. Participants volunteer to take a graduate course which meets one evening a week for 3 hours. Class meetings follow a full day of work, and attention is difficult for even the most dedicated teachers. But since the effectiveness of the project relies on classroom implementation of the concepts and instructional strategies learned in class, summer courses are no substitute for those conducted during the academic year.

While gaining released time for teachers is not easy, it is necessary if significant changes are to be made in mathematics instruction. In our hypothetical model the planning team will find ways to make released time available. Practical ways might include imaginative scheduling, use of adopt-a-school programs, financial supplements from funding agencies, and the like. At the time of writing, the FWISD mathematics project was planning its advanced course for teacher trainers as a summer offering conducted in conjunction with a program for mathematically able youngsters. This arrangement, however, is intended to supplement staff development during the academic year, not to supplant it.

Once a timetable for staff development is established, teachers must begin to address the question of curriculum, for curriculum is the medium of learning. Under the guidance of the district's Director of Mathematics, the teachers in our hypothetical model will thoroughly study the K–12 curriculum recommended by the National Council of Teachers of Mathematics. The university mathematics educator will familiarize the teachers with research on how students learn mathematics. This research will provide the basis for designing learning environments that move students through the curriculum yet respect their individual differences—for example, variations in ability, background, and motivation.

During their year of preparation, the teachers will revamp the school district's K–12 mathematics curriculum in accordance with NCTM standards. In addition, they will develop an instructional framework that allows students to progress as rapidly as their abilities and interests dictate. Before they can design such a framework, the teachers must agree on the nature of mathematical thinking and the conditions which foster it. Here again, the NCTM publication on programs for the mathematically gifted provides guidance:

> Any program for gifted and talented students must have academic integrity. Students should be held accountable for knowing more because they are in a special program, and the content they are expected to know must have more substance than piecemeal topics of mere curiosity (House, 1987, p. 32).

In an earlier *Agenda for Action,* the National Council of Teachers of Mathematics identified problem solving as the most important goal for mathematics instruction (NCTM, 1980, p. 2). In its more recent *Curriculum and Evaluation Standards for School Mathematics,* the NCTM keeps problem solving at the center of the curriculum: "Not only is the ability to solve problems a major reason for studying mathematics, but problem solving provides a context in which concepts and skills can be learned" (Commission, 1988, p. 22). Since problem solving emphasizes high-order thinking skills, it constitutes an appropriate vehicle for organizing a mathematics curriculum for able learners. It cannot be assumed, however, that mathematically talented youngsters take naturally to problem solving. Again, the advice of NCTM:

> Many very bright youngsters have no sense of how to address problems that are new to them, even though they do their standard schoolwork exceptionally well. Many, if presented with a problem that they cannot answer immediately, respond with withdrawal (House, 1987, p.32).

Good mathematical problems usually involve several areas of mathematics and can be easily extended. Consequently it is important that both learning environments and pacing be sufficiently flexible to allow students to make decisions about their learning experiences. Gifted students show improved academic achievement and better self-concepts when they are allowed choices and some control over their own learning (Clark, 1983).

At the conclusion of their year of preparation, the teachers in our hypothetical model should possess a full understanding of the concepts constituting a K–12 mathematics curriculum and should be proficient in developing problem-solving environments. They will then be ready to assume leadership as teacher trainers in their respective schools.

Programmatic changes, both curricular and instructional, must be implemented within existing structures. Therefore, we will first establish continuous progress separately in elementary school, in middle school, and in high school. We will then consider the transition between these educational entities. Traditionally, specific mathematical concepts have been tied to specific grades. Since grades are tied to age, the concepts are tied to age. In our continuous progress model, the concepts will be tied to ability and to motivation. Each teacher will be assigned a group of children based on the mathematics concepts for which the students are ready. When a student has mastered all of the concepts taught by that teacher, she will be reassigned to a teacher responsible for the next group of concepts on the continuum. Teachers will rotate concepts periodically to assure their familiarity with various levels of mathematical thinking and to reinforce an awareness of relationships among concepts. Scheduling will be arranged so that all teachers teach mathematics at the same time.

The FWISD mathematics project argues for the feasibility of the plan described here. Some of the teachers in the project are in schools where all mathematics instruction is scheduled during the same time block. These teachers have entered into cooperative planning that allows each teacher to focus on individual teaching strengths and to share those strengths with other teachers. Scheduling in blocks enables students to move from one teacher to another without significant disruption. This experience suggests that well trained teachers provided with appropriate scheduling of mathematics classes may naturally increase flexibility in their classrooms. Since it is unlikely that flexibility will occur without such support systems, staff development and appropriate scheduling are a sine qua non of our hypothetical model.

All teachers at all grade levels will be required to participate in inservice training equivalent to a graduate course. Such training is best conducted in the summer prior to initiating continuous progress. The Director of Mathematics and the university mathematics educator will work closely with the instructional leaders from the schools to structure the training. Initially elementary teachers, middle school teachers, and high school teachers will meet separately, each group studying those concepts most likely to be taught in their setting. Teams of teachers formed within each school will bear responsibility for specific groups of concepts. The teachers will also examine learning environments and instructional strategies that facilitate the teaching of those concepts.

The lockstep approach to teaching mathematics has been most problematic in the transitional grades: fifth grade elementary and sixth grade middle school, eighth grade middle and ninth grade high school. That repetition in these grades results in boredom for students at these times is borne out by the survey of student attitudes conducted at Las Cruces (see Chapter 5 on Flexible Pacing at All Levels). Since one goal of staff development is to ensure that the mathematical progress of students is not impaired during critical transition, teachers formerly assigned to these interfacing grades, now assigned to interfacing mathematics concepts, will participate in joint staff development.

Approximately two-thirds of the way through the inservice preparation, the teachers at these interfacing grades will form groups, elementary and middle school teachers in one group, middle and high school teachers in another group. These teachers will explore ways to move students from one school to another when their progress indicates a readiness for transition. This will be particularly critical in the initial move from elementary school to middle school. High school teachers will also examine early college concepts and curricula.

Again, the FWISD mathematics project lends support to our hypothetical model. A Title II grant under the Educational Economic Security Act enabled the school district to bring together 19 teachers from the elementary, middle, and high school levels to focus on current issues in mathematics education. For the first time these teachers had an opportunity to share perspectives, problems, and solutions to problems. Illustrating from their own teaching experiences, they

> *Transitions could be eased for students if*
> *the teachers were knowledgeable about the*
> *whole curriculum and if students were provided*
> *more flexibility of pacing within*
> *and between grades.*

reiterated the difficulties encountered by students in transitional grades. They also affirmed that these transitions could be eased for students if the teachers at these grade levels were knowledgeable about the whole curriculum and if students were provided more flexibility of pacing within and between grades.

Since staff development within and between grade levels must be ongoing, even during the implementation of the hypothetical model, scheduled planning time will enable teaching teams to meet every week. As other feeder systems in the school district begin their staff development, the initial feeder system will provide on-site training. Instructional leaders of the initial feeder system will be released from some teaching assignments to assist in the staff development for other feeder systems. Even after all schools in the district have installed continuous progress in mathematics, selected teachers will continue to explore teaching strategies that facilitate the mathematical progress of students.

While staff development is the key consideration in the reform of mathematics education, other considerations must be addressed— textbooks, for example, and other teaching materials. The Second International Mathematics Study found that

> the student textbook was clearly the most consistently used resource in teaching . . . . Other materials seldom appeared as a primary source and were rarely or never used by 75–80% of the teachers. This was true even in areas such as geometry and measurement in which such materials might be considered most helpful (Crosswhite, et al., 1985, p. 14).

Rigid adherence to textbooks relates to another finding of the study: "Teachers tended to be symbolic and formal rather than intuitive and concrete." Because mathematics textbooks fail to ground their principles in concrete experience, staff development must encourage teachers to overcome their dependence on textbooks. Teachers will be exposed to the myriad instructional resources for mathematics

---

*Because mathematics textbooks fail to ground
their principles in concrete experience, staff
development must encourage teachers to
overcome their dependence on textbooks.*

---

currently available from supply houses such as Creative Publications and Cuisenaire Company of America.

Using concrete manipulative materials in teaching mathematics can provide a way of involving parents more directly in the instructional process. Good materials such as pattern blocks, Cuisenaire rods, and geoboards invite investigation. Children often ask to take these manipulatives home overnight. Impressed with the involvement of their children, parents then want more information about how such materials are helping their children learn mathematics.

Keeping parents informed cannot be left entirely in the hands of teachers. Information can be provided through a school's parent-teacher organization or at a mathematics fair. Parents can be encouraged to purchase mathematics manipulatives for their children. Since the cost of these materials is prohibitive for some families, the school library might purchase them. In some communities the public library might be persuaded to house a collection of mathematics materials.

Recently several excellent videotape series have have been produced which demonstrate concrete instructional modes for introducing children to higher level mathematical thinking. Marilyn Burns (1988) and Seymour Papert (1987), both well-known mathematics educators, have been involved in such series. The videotapes are invaluable for staff development and, because of the increasing popularity of home videoplayers, can be circulated among interested parents. Philosophical frameworks as well as classroom strategies are coherently presented.

A final area of concern, although certainly not the least in the long line of consideration, is assessment. Education today suffers under the tyranny of standardized testing. Testing programs have become so powerful and so pervasive that they are likely to determine the curriculum rather than the reverse. The tests themselves have a skewed focus. A recent position of the National Council of Supervisors of Mathematics illustrates the seriousness of the situation:

> Nationally-normed standardized tests that are currently in use do not match the objectives of a mathematics curriculum designed to

---

*Teachers must encounter assessment modes
that are not so heavily reliant on pencil and
paper, but attend more to observation
and application.*

---

designed to prepare students for the 21st century. The focus of testing must shift from computation to problem solving and reasoning. At this time the use of standardized tests to monitor student progress and evaluate the effectiveness of instruction is harmful. Existing standardized tests perpetuate the domination of the mathematics curriculum by lower-order skills, and their results give a false sense of accomplishment (NCSM, 1988, p. 4).

To counter over-reliance on standardized testing, the planning team must be particularly aggressive in helping teachers to identify or develop assessment instruments that are diagnostic in nature and aligned with the new curriculum. Written tests frequently attend only to the products of learning, ignoring the processes that lead to the attainment of the products. Teachers must encounter assessment modes that are not so heavily reliant on pencil and paper, but attend more to observation and application. Such modes will free them from the time-consuming task of correcting papers and allow them time to reflect on the intellectual and personal qualities that underlie learning.

The NCTM position on assessment is that testing methods should reflect a diversity of instructional methods and the various ways students come to know. At the same time, testing must allow for diversity of student responses (House, 1987).

Staff development, curriculum design, new teaching methods, use of manipulatives, testing—these elements make up a crowded agenda. Real experience, however, suggests that the agenda is more stimulating than daunting. Teachers at all levels are eager to learn, to try out new approaches, to become better teachers. Undoubtedly the planning team will encounter additional challenges as it puts in place a curriculum that provides for the continuous mathematical progress of students. When such challenges occur, cooperation of all constituencies remains the key to success. The Mathematical Sciences Education Board is right. Without such cooperation, no curriculum project, no matter how well conceived, will succeed.

CHAPTER 9

Conclusion

Most of this study of flexible pacing for able learners has been descriptive rather than prescriptive. We have looked at real programs in place around the country and have not tried to suggest we have a theoretical bombshell. Nor have we offered an agenda for action. We start with the belief that the best education takes place when new concepts, new content, are presented in a way and at a pace that fits diverse learning rates and learning styles. Insofar as we may influence educational change, it will be by presenting a view of what is going on where educators share our belief and by showing a range of options from which schools and districts can select what appears most sensible and apt for imitation.

And yet, our prejudice in favor of flexible pacing has been reinforced by seeing how it is managed in a variety of settings and by reading the testimonials of those who practice flexible pacing as well as those who are its beneficiaries. We have read and tried to share many insights about how flexible pacing is achieved. A predictable consequence is that this slim volume has become both an argument for flexible pacing and a primer of sorts. While it makes no case for a single method or even a unitary approach, it offers a number of practical suggestions.

In line with this direction of our essay, we take this opportunity to abstract from the material some of the principles that inform the best practices we have found at work. We'll summarize and conclude by talking about the benefits to be derived from a sound program of flexible pacing and by highlighting selected elements of implementation that deserve reiteration.

The educational benefit of a commitment to flexible pacing is that it individualizes instruction and learning to a higher degree than is

*In a school with continuous progress, students
can move ahead naturally, as they are ready,
and the faster learners need not be jumped
ahead by full-grade intervals, skipping crucial
material, because they are ahead
of their age-mates.*

possible when students all move in lockstep. Particularly at those schools where scheduling has been arranged in blocks to permit an easy flow of students from group to group studying the same subject at different levels, the abler students have found a more steady challenge and less repetition. Once the grade labels have been removed from the achievement levels, and especially if the achievement levels have been dissociated from chronological age, even the more nearly average students have benefited. Neither slowed unnaturally nor pressured to accelerate by the learning rates of their age mates, students of all abilities appear to thrive.

Because we have focused our attention on the more able students, our accounts of achievement have generally been expressed in terms of acceleration. We have tried not to suggest, however, that we favor unbridled acceleration. Mastery of concepts and skills is the point of sound teaching and learning, whatever the pace. One of the benefits of flexible pacing is that it increases the options for every student. In a school with continuous progress, students can move ahead naturally, as they are ready, and the faster learners need not be jumped ahead by full-grade intervals, skipping crucial material, because they are ahead of their age-mates.

The context of what students are learning and the sequence of concepts is crucial to flexible pacing. Artificial barriers should be eliminated. This principle is reflected in the survey of accelerated students in Las Cruces. It should be no surprise that the students surveyed found mathematics, science, and English most repetitive and most boring in grades 5–8. These school years are set off by the boundaries of middle school, boundaries that may make sense as a means of harnessing bodies, but have no justification if they interrupt intellectual growth.

We have mentioned from time to time the benefits experienced by schools that practice some form of flexible pacing. Aside from the benefit of having students more fully engaged in their schoolwork, the schools we have surveyed typically report a high level of involvement from parents and the community. School districts and schools are inevitably and necessarily political organizations, depending on public support for more than money. Good news and public exposure enable a school or district to draw on community resources: cultural institutions, civic organizations, the private sector. Academic competitions and prize scholarships make happy news for any community. Insofar as flexible pacing may contribute to or increase such achievements, it makes a welcome contribution. But even more, because flexible pacing requires consent, cooperation, and involvement from the parents of students in such a program, it enlists their energies and their commitment. No other commodity is so precious to education.

Flexible pacing, of course, entails flexible instruction and flexible management of the educational enterprise. Putting a program in place also requires a limberness and adaptability that will test the most resilient institutions. We return to the issue of implementation in the belief that the gains are worth the effort.

Our chapter on Selected Features of Flexible Pacing offers a kind of checklist for a school or district moving toward flexible pacing. It begins with the importance of developing a district or school policy that encourages flexible pacing. It mentions the populations typically served by the programs we have surveyed, making the point that while only a small percentage of students are noticeably accelerated, all benefit from the increased individualization. The chapter also points out that school districts start where they most easily can, with one school in a district or with one subject in the curriculum. Our list of features that characterize the successful schools includes attention to staff development, record keeping, and methods of evaluation. It ends with the importance of support mechanism, which returns us to the politics of implementation.

The principles that bob up through our discussion of how flexible pacing is "done" include capitalizing on whatever is available. Opportunism is a virtue in education. For example, new developments in educational technology, including software that eases record keeping, are making it relatively simple to keep track of students' progress even when the students advance at different rates. Providing supplementary materials in alternative media relieves some of the headache of keeping up with the student whose learning rate or special interests do not fit the conventional mold. The professional literature and other specialized publications are full of ideas for varying student groups, for team teaching, for special projects.

Another sense of starting with what is available includes initiating a program of flexible pacing a little at a time. As we recommended in a previous publication (Cox, Daniel, & Boston, 1985), a comprehensive program for all students or any selected group of students can be put together like a mosaic, piece by piece. Flexible pacing is one piece,

*A comprehensive program for all students
or any selected group of students can be put
together like a mosaic, piece by piece.*

probably a piece to put in early. Start wherever a start can be made: with a single subject, with a single set of students, with a single school. Small improvements, when successful, garner support.

Winning support is perhaps the crucial element in all the success stories we have uncovered at schools with flexible pacing. Corollary to winning support is a spirit of cooperation that characterizes the best efforts in education. A theme that runs through all we have said is that collaboration is essential to success. Our chapter on Cooperative Programs pays special attention to the need for joint effort between schools, throughout communities, among the various sectors of society, across the traditional boundaries that segment our national school system.

That we should urge cooperation and united effort as we argue for individualizing education is a paradox without irony. The metaphor in our introduction, a cable of many strands, is an emblem for the kind of education we recommend. An education that allows each student to move through the curriculum as that student masters skills and concepts must contain as many filaments as there are students. And as we have suggested, even the single student learns at different rates, often by different means, in each separate subject.

What it takes to conceive and establish such an education is a complex effort also made of many individual and quite discrete contributions. The larger the district, the more complicated the task. But there is no other way.

References

(Note: Throughout the book we refer to the individuals who responded to our survey, quoting passages from their responses, summarizing information in their documents. These contributors are listed separately in an appendix and are not included in the list of references.)

Anderson, R. H., & Goodlad, J. I. (1962). Self-appraisal in nongraded schools: A survey of findings and perceptions. *The Elementary School Journal, 62*(5), 261–269.

Benbow, C. C., & Stanley, J. C. (1983). Constructing educational bridges between high school and college. *Gifted Child Quarterly, 27*(3), 111–113.

Burns, M. (1988). *Mathematics with manipulatives.* New Rochelle, NY: Cuisenaire Company of America.

Clark, B. (1983). *Growing up gifted: Developing the potential of children at home and at school* (2nd ed.). Columbus, OH: Charles E. Merrill.

Commission on Standards for School Mathematics of the National Council of Teachers of Mathematics. (1988). *Curriculum and evaluation standards for school mathematics.* Reston, VA: National Council of Teachers of Mathematics.

Cox, J., Daniel, N., & Boston, B. O. (1985). *Educating able learners: Programs and promising practices.* Austin: University of Texas Press.

Crosswhite, J., Dossey, J., Swafford, J., McKnight, C., & Cooney, T. (1985). *Second international mathematics study summary report for the United States.* Champaign, IL: Stripes Publishing.

Daurio, S. P. (1979). Educational enrichment versus acceleration: A review of the literature. In W. C. George, S. J. Cohn, & J. C. Stanley (Eds.), *Educating the gifted: Acceleration and enrichment* (pp. 13–63). Baltimore: The Johns Hopkins University Press.

Feldman, R. D. (1985, October). The Pyramid Project. *Instructor, 62–66,* 71.

Fox, E. (1985). International schools and the International Baccalaureate. *Harvard Educational Review, 55,* 53–68.

Gallagher, J. J. (1985a). *Teaching the gifted child* (3rd ed.). Boston: Allyn and Bacon.

Gallagher, J. J. (1985b). Educational strategies for gifted students in secondary schools. *NASSP Bulletin* (National Association of Secondary School Principals), *69*(482), 17–24.

Gardner, H. (1983). *Frames of mind: The theory of multiple intelligences.* New York: Basic Books.

Goldberg, M., & Passow, A. H. (1966). The effects of ability grouping. In A. Morgenstern (Ed.), *Grouping in elementary school* (pp. 22–39). New York: Pitman.

Goodlad, J., & Anderson, R. (1959). *The nongraded elementary school.* New York: Harcourt Brace.

Gross, M. (1986, July/August). Radical acceleration in Australia: Terence Tao. *G/C/T*, 2–11.

House, P. (Ed.). (1987). *Providing opportunities for the mathematically gifted*. Reston, VA: National Council of Teachers of Mathematics.

Hunter, M. (1964). The dimensions of nongrading. *The Elementary School Journal*, 65(1): 20–25.

Kulik, J. A., & Kulik, C. C. (1984). Synthesis of research on effects of accelerated instruction. *Educational Leadership*, 42, 84–89.

Maeroff, G. I. (1983). *School and college: Partnerships in education*. Princeton: Carnegie Foundation for the Advancement of Teaching.

Mathematical Sciences Education Board Curriculum Task Force. (1987). *A philosophy and framework for the K–12 mathematics curriculum*. Unpublished working paper.

Miller, R. I. (1967). The nongraded movement: Historical and sociological perspectives. In R. I. Miller (Ed.), *The nongraded school: Analysis and study* (pp. 1–15). New York: Harper & Row.

Morgenstern, A. (1966). Historical survey of grouping practices in the elementary school. In A. Morgenstern (Ed.), *Grouping in the elementary school* (pp. 3–13). New York: Pitman.

Naisbitt, J. (1984). *Megatrends: Ten new directions transforming our lives*. New York: Warner Books.

National Council of Supervisors of Mathematics. (1988). *Basic mathematics skills for the 21st century*. Minneapolis, MN: National Council of Supervisors of Mathematics. Draft position paper.

National Council of Teachers of Mathematics. (1980). *An agenda for action*. Reston, VA: National Council of Teachers of Mathematics.

Olson, L. (1987). Network for renewal: Goodlad seeks stronger school-university alliances. *Education Week*, 6(25), 1, 18.

Papert, S. (1987). *On Logo*. St. Louis, MO: Media Microworks.

Renzulli, J. S. (1977). *The enrichment triad model*. Mansfield, CT: Creative Learning Press.

Robinson, N. M., & Robinson, H. B. (1982). The optimal match: Devising the best compromise for the highly gifted student. In D. Feldman (Ed.), *Developmental approaches to giftedness and creativity* (pp. 79–94). San Francisco: Jossey-Bass.

Sawyer, R. N. (1984). The Duke University educational programs for brilliant youth. *Roeper Review*, 7(2), 103–109.

Slavin, R. E. (1987). Grouping for instruction in the elementary school. *Educational Psychologist*, 22(2), 109–127.

Snow, R. E. (1986). Individual differences and the design of educational programs. *American Psychologist*, 41(10), 1029–1039.

Stanley, J. C. (1979). Educational non-acceleration: An international tragedy. In J. J. Gallagher (Ed.), *Gifted children: Reaching their potential*. Proceedings of the Third International Conference on Gifted Children (pp. 16–43). Jerusalem, Israel: Kollek & Son.

Stanley, J. C. (1980). On educating the gifted. *Educational Researcher*, 9(3), 8–12.

Toffler, A. (1971). *Future shock*. (Bantam ed.). New York: Bantam.

VanTassel-Baska, J. (1985). The talent search model: Implications for secondary school reform. *NASSP Bulletin* (National Association of Secondary School Principals), *69*(482), 39–47.

VanTassel-Baska, J. (1986). Acceleration. In C. J. Maker (Ed.), *Critial issues in gifted educaton: Defensible programs for the gifted* (pp. 179–196). Rockville, MD: Aspen.

Yale-New Haven Teachers Institute. (1983). *Teaching in America: The common ground.* New Haven, CT: Author.

Appendices

Appendix A
Survey Forms

Flexible Pacing Survey Form Sent to Elementary Schools and to School Districts

School District _____

School _____
      (If you are reporting on an individual school.)

Name of person completing this report _____

Person's title_____ Telephone No. _____

Address _____
              (Street)

_____

    (City)   (State)   (Zip Code)

Number of students in district _____

Number of students in school _____

Number of students in flexible pacing program _____

Specific Questions:

How long has the flexible pacing program been in existence?

_____

What content areas by age and grade levels are represented? _____

_____

_____

How many students regularly receive instruction above their age/ grade level by ____one year? ____two years? ____more than two years?

Is there a board policy that requires, or at least encourages, flexible pacing? ____No ____Yes. If yes, please summarize and attach a copy of policy. _____

_____

_____

Staff Development

Briefly describe any special staff development activities for teachers and administrators in the program. _____

_____

_____

_____

_____

_____

_____

Program Narrative

Describe the program. Explain the administrative arrangements that enable flexible pacing to take place and any special record-keeping techniques that are used to monitor student progress. If this is not a K–12 program, note what type of program students are in before and following the flexible pacing experience. Also, if only one school in the district is involved, explain why you think flexible pacing is not a district-wide practice. _____

_____

_____

_____

_____

_____

Student Case Studies

Describe the experiences of one or more students who have participated in the program, giving special attention to successes or problems encountered while they were in the program and in later schooling. You may wish to comment on their social and emotional development as well as on their academic achievement. _____

_____

_____

_____

_____

_____

Program Evaluation

Describe procedures used to evaluate the program. Also, enclose summaries of evaluation findings and recommendations. _____

_____

_____

_____

_____

_____

Flexible Pacing Survey Form Sent to Secondary Schools

School District _____
School _____
Name of person completing this survey _____
Person's title_____ Telephone No. _____
Address _____
                    (Street)

_____
         (City)   (State)   (Zip Code)

Number of students in district _____
Number of students in school _____
Number of students in flexible pacing options _____

Please check the options that are routinely available in your school or district:

_____ Advanced Placement (College Board)

_____ International Baccalaureate

_____ Concurrent enrollment in lower school and high school

_____ Concurrent enrollment in high school and college

_____ College courses offered on the high school campus

_____ Honors courses (other than AP or IB)

_____ Others (please be as specific as possible)

Program Narrative

Please describe the program (or programs) in your own words. We are interested to know of special administrative arrangements that enable diverse options to take place. If you offer courses that lead to credit by examination, such as AP or IB, do you require or encourage students to take the examinations? If your school is involved in cooperative programs with other institutions or agencies, please explain how such programs are administered. _____

_____

_____

_____
_____
_____
_____

Student Selection

How do students qualify and how are they chosen to participate in accelerated classes or other special programs? _____
_____
_____
_____
_____
_____
_____
_____

Staff Development

Briefly describe any special staff development activities for teachers and administrators in the program. _____
_____
_____
_____
_____
_____
_____

Program Evaluation

Describe procedures used to evaluate the program. Also, please include summaries of evaluation findings and recommendations. ___
_____
_____
_____
_____
_____
_____

Printed Materials

Please send us copies of brochures, printed reports, or official statements that are available for public distribution. We are especially interested in educational philosophy, school board policy, local statutes, or legislative actions that undergird your program for superior students.

Appendix B
The High Pointe Plan

[This document was sent to parents in the Cedar Hill district to explain the innovations at the new school. It reflects the program in its first year and does not incorporate changes made later.]

Cedar Hill Independent School District is currently part of the 5–year Pyramid Project funded by the Sid Richardson Foundation and directed by the Gifted Students Institute of Fort Worth, Texas. This project is based on the results of a 4–year research effort led by June Cox to study "able learners" and the methods used to meet their special needs. One of the recommendations of this study is that students should move ahead as they demonstrate mastery in content areas and skills. The program at High Pointe Elementary incorporates continuous progress, a part of Cox's study, to deliver the district curriculum. Continuous progress permits students to progress at an appropriate rate along a continuum of instructional objectives. Students and/or classes progress through the appropriate curriculum as content mastery is demonstrated. The goal of the High Pointe plan is to provide appropriate instruction that reaches across grade levels and disciplines for all students in all subjects. Cedar Hill Independent School District chose to pilot continuous progress at one elementary school during the 1986–1987 school year.

The daily schedule at High Pointe is divided into three basic learning modules. The three "Timeblocks" represent Reading/Language Arts; Mathematics/Science; and Humanities. Students move along the Reading/Language Arts and Math/Science skills continuum based on performance and achievement. The Humanities Module brings students together in heterogenous groups to explore content areas suitable for cognitive and affective development. This particular module explores fine arts, creative writing, literature, social studies, and physical education. The kindergarten program is self-contained; however, students with unique abilities are allowed to advance when appropriate.

Initial placement of students requires access to the previous year's Criterion Reference Test (R-COBE) scores in language arts and mathematics. With these scores as a basis, students are either pre- or posttested with the R-COBE to ensure proper placement. (R-COBE is the Regional Cooperative for Outcome-Based Instruction.)

The school counselor and staff meet each 6 weeks to review student achievement and to discuss appropriate placement. Parents are notified of all changes before they occur. New students and their parents are interviewed by the counselor. The program is explained in its entirety, and students are assigned "PALS" to help them through their first few days at High Pointe. Both informal and formal testing is done to ensure proper placement. Placement of new students is monitored closely and transfers are made as needed.

While the majority of students at High Pointe work at a traditional level, some are placed "off level." Students often work at different levels in different subject areas. Regardless of the placement, meeting the students' needs is the one and only concern.

Accurate record keeping, easy access to R-COBE results, and the posting of these test results are all vital to the implementation of this program. The Mastery Management System purchased through Region X [Education Service Center] is the vehicle used to accomplish these goals. This system is used to facilitate record keeping of student data and individual class results as well as to provide easy access to the district curriculum objectives and prerequisites. The system produces an individual student profile that is included with the report card. This profile indicates objectives taught, mastered, and not mastered, and also lists those to be taught. With this information, parents are able to see exactly what their child has accomplished or will accomplish.

Creativity and higher-level thinking skills are encouraged, and each student is allowed to develop his/her special talents. Enrichment in content areas is never sacrificed for the sake of moving forward. The media center is structured to complement all areas of the curriculum. Students are encouraged to work on special projects under the direction of the librarian.

Two administrative interns are a part of the High Pointe staff. These interns conduct workshops for staff development, provide instructional leadership, and are used throughout the district to further teacher education. They are also available to assist with the day-to-day operations of the school. The interns will be used in the future to implement continuous progress throughout the district.

Appendix C
Las Cruces Public Schools
Evaluation, AEP

STUDENT CASE STUDIES

By the spring of 1985, the Las Cruces Schools had a population of 16,000 students. Five-hundred-fifty of these students, grades K–12, were placed in the Advanced Education Program. Seventy-one students were in grades 10–12. A study was designed to ascertain student perceptions of the academic and social effects of the acceleration program. A population of 40 accelerated high school students were targeted for the study. A questionnaire was developed which asked 16 questions about the academic effects of acceleration and 11 questions regarding the social effects of acceleration. Thirty-seven completed questionnaires were received.

Sixty-five percent of the respondents in the study were male; 35% were female. Forty-six percent had been accelerated 1–2 years; 54% had been accelerated 3 or more years.

Responses to each section were tabulated and converted to percentages for reporting purposes. Responses were further classified according to sex and years of participation in the program. A chi square test for independence was conducted to determine if there were any significant differences at the .05 level of confidence between perceptions of males and females or between students who have participated in the accelerated program 1–2 years versus 3+ years. No significant differences were found. Students were also asked to elaborate on their responses. These expanded items and responses were examined to provide precision in determining what caused students to select each response.

RESULTS OF THE STUDY

The Academic Effects of Acceleration

The students were asked if acceleration into higher level coursework added more pressure to their academic work, affected their gradepoint, and required more study time.

Gradepoint Average — Fifty-nine percent of the students noted that acceleration into higher level coursework had not caused a change in their gradepoint average. Fourteen percent noted their gradepoint averages had gone up because of an increased interest in school.

Study Time | Fifty-seven percent of the students felt they spent no more time studying following their acceleration than they did before. Of those who did spend more time, 14% noted that more time was required because part of their acceleration coursework now included college level work.

Increase in Pressure | Seventy-one percent of the male students noted no increase in pressure from acceleration while 62% of the females did feel an increase. An analysis of anecdotal reponses indicated females pressured themselves to make the top grades and felt some peer pressure because of being a "brain."

Productive Years | The students were also asked to analyze which years in school and which academic courses had been so repetitive as to cause them to lose interest in school. Math, English, and science in grades 5–8 were seen by the students to have been the least satisfactory, nonproductive courses, and years. Repetition of previously learned coursework was cited by the students as the reasons for considering these subjects and grades their nonproductive years.

A minority of students did feel some negative academic effects of their acceleration. Fifty-nine percent of the students felt an increase in pressure to excel from some of their teachers following their placement in the accelerated program. Ten students had a drop in gradepoint average following their acceleration. Sixteen students had to increase their amount of study time because of being enrolled in more complex coursework at an earlier age.

The Social Effects of Acceleration

The students were asked to make judgments on how acceleration had affected their social lives while in school.

Social Life | The majority of the students, 95%, felt they had an average to excellent social life. Sixty-seven percent felt that their acceleration had not caused their social life to differ from their nonaccelerated peers. Of those who did see a difference in their social life, these reasons were cited as causes for the difference: one student felt his social life differed because he had ties in two schools; four students felt their social lives differed because of a choice not to party with some of their peers; only two students saw a difference in their social life because they were younger than their classmates.

Friends

Ninety-two percent of the accelerated students viewed themselves as having "several" to "many" friends. Students overwhelmingly enjoyed the widened friendship groups that came with acceleration into higher-level coursework with older students. A change in allegiance to friends was noted as students continued their acceleration over a number of years. Students who had been in the accelerated program only 1 or 2 years identified more with their same age friends. Students who had been in the accelerated program 3 years or more identified more with their older friends.

Extracurricular Activities

Almost all of the accelerated students, 95%, balanced their academic life with memberships in clubs, sports, or other activities outside of school. About half of these students held positions of leadership in these clubs or other outside activities.

Recommendations

The students were asked for comments they would make to other students, who might be considering acceleration, concerning the effects it would have on their social life. Ninety percent of the students recommended acceleration as the finding of new friends had enhanced their social lives. Some of their comments were: "My friendship group has widened as I've added new, older friends." "Acceleration doesn't make or break friends—you do!"

CONCLUSION: "WOULD YOU DO IT OVER AGAIN?"

The responses of all the students studied indicated they felt far more positive than negative effects from their acceleration. They felt that the opportunity for early entry into more complex curricular structures, and thus elimination of some of the repetition built into the public school curriculum had greatly enhanced their academic lives. They viewed their accelerated years as more productive, challenging years.

One hundred percent of the students felt that if they had the choice to make over again, they would still choose to accelerate. The advantages far outweighed any disadvantages.

Some of the students' summary statements regarding acceleration were:

"You'll have to work harder and make new friends, but it's worth it."

"I feel as if I don't have to sit with my hands down any longer."

Appendix D
Contributors

This list includes those who returned the survey forms from the schools indicated. Because up to 2 years have passed since the forms were returned, some persons have moved or changed positions. The contributors are listed in the order in which their schools are mentioned in the text.

Keith P. Langford Principal	Lowell Elementary School Salt Lake City School District Salt Lake City, Utah
Marcy Mager Principal	New Durham Elementary School Governor Wentworth Regional School District New Durham, New Hampshire.
Jane G. Fox Principal	Friendsville Elementary School Garrett County Public Schools Friendsville, Maryland
Cathy Coulter, Principal Nancy Plato, Lead Teacher	Irving Alternative School Sioux Falls Public Schools Sioux Falls, South Dakota
Thomas E. Rowan, Elementary Mathematics Coordinator	Montgomery County Public Schools Rockville, Maryland
Larry E. Howard Principal	Walter J. Leeper Middle School Claremore Independent School District #1 Claremore, Oklahoma
Mary M. Bray Curriculum Assistant Colleen Passaro, Teacher	Lecanto Primary School Citrus County School District Lecanto, Florida

Joe N. Neely
Superintendent

High Pointe Elementary School
Cedar Hill Independent School
District (Dallas County)
Cedar Hill, Texas

Deanna Broughton
Director of Instruction

Ardmore City Schools District
Ardmore, Oklahoma

Richard H. Tyre
Dean of Academic Programs

Haverford Senior High School
Haverford Township School
District
Havertown, Pennsylvania

Ward J. Ghory
Assistant Principal

Walnut Hills High School
Cincinnati Public Schools
Cincinnati, Ohio

Richard T. Stanley
Assistant Principal

Whitney High School
ABC Unified School District
Cerritos, California

Paul J. Sousa
Principal

Murphy High School
Mobile County School System
Mobile, Alabama

Michael N. Riley
Principal

Middletown High School
Frederick County Board of
Education
Middletown, Maryland

Richard A. Abraham
Counselor

Centennial High School
Independent School District #12
Circle Pines, Minnesota

Richard Morris
Administrative Assistant

Valley High School
Elk Grove Unified School
District
Sacramento, California

Harold J. Dusick
Assistant Principal

Chandler High School
Chandler Unified School District #80
Chandler, Arizona

James E. Kroll
International Baccalaureate Coordinator

Rufus King High School
Milwaukee Public Schools
Milwaukee, Wisconsin

Jim Allison
Gifted Education Coordinator

Jefferson County Public Schools
Golden, Colorado

Dianna M. Lindsay
Principal
Doug Sebring, Coordinator

North Olmsted High School
North Olmsted City Schools
North Olmsted, Ohio

Gary E. Heideman
Director of Gifted Programs

Rockford Public Schools District 205
Rockford, Illinois

Gerry Haggard
Reading Coordinator

Plano Independent School District
Plano, Texas

Bob Windham
Principal

Ruth Ditto Elementary School
Arlington Independent School District
Arlington, Texas

Margaret Russell
Instructional Consultant

Arlington Independent School District
Arlington, Texas

Barbara Morrison
Advanced Education Program Facilitator

Las Cruces Public Schools
Las Cruces, New Mexico

Sharon Higham
Director of Academic Programs
Carol J. Mills
Coordinator for Young Students

Center for the Advancement of Academically Talented Youth (CTY)
The Johns Hopkins University
Baltimore, Maryland.

Richard C. Miller
Supervisor of Gifted Programs

Appalachia Intermediate Unit 8
Hollidaysburg Area School
District
Spring Cove School District
Hollidaysburg, Pennsylvania

David P. Hermanson
GATE Administrator

San Diego Unified School
District
San Diego, California

Bryan L. Moore
Director of Curriculum and
Pupil Services

Indian Hill Exempted Village
School District
Cincinnati, Ohio

James Hill
Department Chairperson

North Central High School
Metropolitan School District of
Washington Township
Indianapolis, Indiana

David A. Goodwill
Coordinator

Kenwood Academy
Chicago Public Schools
Chicago, Illinois

John T. Lewy
Principal

Mast Way Elementary School
Oyster River Cooperative School
District
Durham, New Hampshire